HOPE IN THE MADNESS

WALKING OUT OF ADDICTION AND INTO THE FREEDOM YOU DESIRE

GARY ACKERT

ILLUMIFY MEDIA GLOBAL
Littleton, Colorado

Hope in the Madness
Copyright © 2020 by Gary Ackert

All rights reserved. No part of this book may be reproduced in any form or by any means—whether electronic, digital, mechanical, or otherwise—without permission in writing from the publisher, except by a reviewer, who may quote brief passages in a review.

The views and opinions expressed in this book are those of the author and do not necessarily reflect the official policy or position of Illumify Media Global.

All Scripture quotations are taken from the NEW AMERICAN STANDARD BIBLE®, Copyright © 1960, 1962, 1963, 1968, 1971, 1972, 1973, 1975, 1977, 1995 by The Lockman Foundation. Used by permission.

Published by
Illumify Media Global
www.IllumifyMedia.com
"Write. Publish. Market. *SELL!*"

Library of Congress Control Number: 2020907291

Paperback ISBN: 978-1-947360-40-2
eBook ISBN: 978-1-947360-41-9

Cover design by Debbie Lewis

Printed in the United States of America

CONTENTS

Acknowledgments . . .
Introduction . . .

Chapter 1: What Is Addiction? . . . 1
How Does Addiction Work? . . . 3
Consequences of Addiction . . . 7

Chapter 2: God Still Loves the Mess We're In . . . 11
God Does Care About His Creation . . . 16
God Loves His Creation . . . 17

Chapter 3: We Are Created in God's Image . . . 23
Created in God's Image: We Can Think . . . 24
Created in God's Image: We Can Feel . . . 25
Created in God's Image: We Make Choices . . . 25

Created in God's Image - We Are Made to Live in Relationship . . . 26
We Think . . . 28
We Feel . . . 33
We Make Choices . . . 35
We Live in Relationship . . . 37

Chapter 4: Our World Is Broken . . . 41
Sin Broke Everything . . . 42
Our Relationship with God Is Broken . . . 43
Addiction makes sense 45
Our Relationships with Others Are Broken . . . 46
Our Relationship with Self Is Broken . . . 47
Sin Broke the Image of God Within Us . . . 47
Our Thoughts Toward God Changed . . . 48
Our Feelings Toward God Changed . . . 48
Our Choices Toward God Changed . . . 49
Our Relationship with God Was Changed . . . 50
Our Relationships with Others Changed . . . 51
Our Relationship with Self Changed . . . 52
My Story . . . 54

Chapter 5: Is This All We Can Hope For? . . . 59
What to Do with Sin? . . . 61
The Gospel Is God's Answer to Sin . . . 61
Jesus Christ: God's Plan and Our Only Hope . . . 63
How Can I Get What the Gospel Offers for My Life? . . . 66

Chapter 6: What Happens Now? . . . 77
God Becomes Lord and King in Our Lives . . . 78

Being in Awe and Reverence . . . 79
God's Will for Every Believer . . . 81
We Are Forgiven . . . 82
We Are No Longer Outcasts . . . 85
We Don't Have to Feel Condemned Anymore . . . 85
We Are Accepted . . . 87
We Are Wanted by God . . . 88
We Are Redeemed . . . 90
We Are Restored . . . 91
A New Way to See Life . . . 92

Chapter 7: Who's with Me? . . . 107
We Are not Alone . . . 108
God Is with Us . . . 110
Jesus Is with Us . . . 112
The Holy Spirit Is with Us . . . 114
A Personal Side Note . . . 115
We Become Part of the Church . . . 117
We Are Loved Unconditionally . . . 120
We Have Hope . . . 122

Chapter 8: The Journey Continues . . . 137

Gospel Outline . . . 141
Notes . . . 142
About the Author . . . 143

To all my friends, clients, support group members, and all my co-workers who have impacted my life I say thank you. It is because of all of you that this book has been made possible. May this book bring hope to all whose lives are impacted by addiction.

ACKNOWLEDGMENTS

First, and foremost, I must acknowledge God for making this book possible. This book has changed from when I started it as God has worked in my life. He has walked with me as I've learned more about addiction, myself, and my story. God has taught me more about His grace, mercy, and love than I could've ever imagined. His patience with me has laid a solid foundation for my life as He continues to redeem, renew, and restore His image in me and His relationship with me.

There are many others I also want to thank. Thank you to all my past clients. You have taught me more than you'll ever know about addiction and how to love. Jen Clark, your patience with this book has been appreciated more than you know. Your ability to work with me to "get it right" has been a blessing. To my pastors, Larry Renoe and Nick Lillo, your contribution has been critical. You both have listened to me, counseled me, and encouraged me along this journey. You've both been an inspiration and a blessing. To Hank, my first therapist, thank you for "chasing after" me when I wanted to quit and give up. Without your running after me that night from your office I would have quit, and this book would never have been written. To my next therapists, Matthew and Clint, if you both hadn't been faithful to call me out on my stuff, this book wouldn't have been written either. To Mark Faggion, Paul Strickland, Bob Arbaugh, and Jonathan Tyler, four friends that, whether you know it or not, have had a profound impact on this book simply by being the friends you are to me. Mark, if it hadn't been for the trip to Toronto, I may have never started this journey. Paul and Bob, I think back over all that we went through together and I get encouraged by it. Jon, our conversations about the gospel and the atonement have helped my clarify my vision and perspective while writing this book. To my wife, Lynda, what can I say. If not for your "gentle" pushing, your confidence in me, and your constant support I never would have pursued this book. Your love for me is incredible.

Thank you all,

Gary

INTRODUCTION

Addiction. Few words are as polarizing as this word. Sides are taken and battle lines are drawn when it comes to defining and describing what addiction is. Some say it is a choice. After all, those addicted must make a choice to use the substance and put it into their bodies; no one forces them to use. Some say it is a disease that affects how the brain works. It changes the way the brain functions and the way decisions are made. Some, like myself, say it's both a disease and a choice. I agree with addiction specialist Dr. Kevin McCauley, who defines addiction as "a disease of choice" in his documentary *Pleasure Unwoven*.[1]

No matter which side you fall on, the results of addiction are always the same. Addiction breaks lives. It devastates the lives of those who suffer from addictions. Plans are lost and dreams die. Addiction makes it easier for people to believe the lies about who they are—their worth and value. Addiction strips them of any sense of dignity or self-respect. Many begin to think that this life of pain and misery is all there is and all they deserve. They lose hope for a better life. For some, addiction becomes their only option to deal with life's uncertainty, pain, and heartache.

Addiction breaks the relationships between those who suffer from addictions and their family members and friends. Trust is lost because people who suffer from addiction often break their promises to get clean, which causes additional heartache. Some steal from family members and friends, and most all of us take advantage of people in order to feed our addiction. Family members and friends become objects used by those who suffer from addictions to get what they want, when they want it, where they want it, and how they want it. The self-centered attitude of those who suffer from addiction drives many people away because they can't take it anymore. It hurts too much to be around those who suffer from addictions.

I work as a licensed addiction counselor (LAC) and licensed professional counselor (LPC) seeing firsthand how addiction breaks people on a daily basis. Seeing the broken lives of men and women who suffer from addiction is difficult to watch. Listening to the stories of lives lost and relationships broken, as well as the disheartening stories of abandonment and isolation breaks my heart. Sometimes it makes me feel like I want to quit—just throw my hands up and walk away. But I know I can't because of what God has done for me personally. He loves all those who suffer from addictions.

My own journey into addiction started early. I was sexually abused and introduced to pornography at a young age. I became addicted to pornography by the time I was in junior high school. I also believed I wasn't good enough for anyone, so I spiraled into a cycle of shame that crippled me.

I believed I couldn't measure up to anyone's expectations, so why try? Yet, I still had to try. If I succeeded, then I always managed to sabotage it; thus, proving I was the failure I believed I was. When I failed, it served to reinforce what I already believed about myself. This led me into a cycle where I feared I would never achieve success or have healthy relationships; this fear addiction was all consuming! Over the years, I developed many more addictions that forced me into a life of isolation.

I was oblivious to my addictions for many years. I couldn't understand why others found what they wanted in life (so I thought) and I couldn't. I wondered why all my relationships with women fell apart. I always felt unloved, rejected, and abandoned by those who mattered most. I was a "once a month friend" for so many people; it felt like no one wanted me around.

Eventually I got married and had a family, but that didn't stop my addictions. I declared bankruptcy (and dragged my family down with me) because of my addiction to the fear of not being good enough. This mind-set crippled me and almost destroyed my family.

There were many who saw what I was doing and spoke up, but I didn't listen to them. I hurt so many well-intentioned people, but I couldn't see what I was doing to them. Eventually I gave up on myself too, because it seemed everyone else had. But there was One who didn't give up on me. That someone was, and still is, God.

Even though I had devastated my life and those around me, God never gave up on me. He continued to pursue me, even when I didn't pursue Him. God's love for me, His grace, and His mercy, carried me through the worst of times.

God brought me to a point where I had to face myself—my addictions, fear, and shame. My journey into recovery started in 1995. I went to a conference in Toronto with a friend. It was there that I started to accept I was addicted to many things. Since then, the road has been long and hard, but well worth it. There have been many relapses and ups and downs, but through it all I have been able to find the life I've been looking for.

I've learned that the life I have longed for can only be found in the Gospel of Jesus Christ. God's grace and mercy, as expressed in the Gospel, friends, family, and my counselors, has helped my find a life I never thought I could or would. Through the Gospel I have found a life of meaning, value, and worth. God is continually teaching me about His love for me and is helping me learn to accept the love of others. I'm constantly reminded that I have inherent value, worth, and dignity because God has created me in His image.

Unfortunately, this is not the story many of us who suffer from addictions learn or hear. Too often, the story we hear is that we have no value or worth. Many times the words we hear are: "send them to detox," "Send them to rehab" or "Send them to jail. Let's just get rid of them." Many times family members and friends give up on us because they can't bear the pain we bring into their lives. They lose any hope that we can or might change. Sometimes they wonder if we even want to change.

Society, hospitals, law enforcement, and sometimes even the church can treat those who suffer from addictions with disrespect. Many ERs look at caring for the intoxicated homeless as wasted bed space. Police become hardened as they try to admit intoxicated individuals into a detox facility. Officers withstand so much abuse from belligerent people, especially physical, that they become numbed to the people they are transporting. Many churches won't work with the homeless or those who suffer from addictions for fear of them "stinking up the joint." They can't see the person behind the stench.

Family members and friends are not immune either. They tire of hoping for a change that never comes and the empty promises that become our standard practice. Many grow weary and don't know what to do to help. Everything they try fails to bring change. Many well-meaning people throw up their hands and say, "To hell with you. I can't take it anymore." They cut off contact because of the hurt and pain. They want to believe in their loved one's or friend's recovery, but the reality of the situation leaves them hopeless.

I feel God urged me to write this book to provide a sense of hope for all who suffer from addictions. The Gospel contains God's response to those who suffer from addictions and those affected by it. God's answer is His mercy, grace, and love expressed in the life and death of Jesus Christ.

God's heart breaks over the broken lives, pain, guilt, and shame we all suffer. He longs for us to know how much He loves us and wants us to return home—like the prodigal son Jesus spoke of in Luke 15:11–32. In this parable, the son decides to leave and follow his own way (addictions, if you will). He goes through a series of hard times and comes to the realization that what he thought he wanted doesn't satisfy him. Eventually, he decides to go home, but as a servant, not a son. The father sees him and rejoices in his return. He refuses to see him as a servant, but as his son.

He throws a huge party, adorns the son in his best clothes, and celebrates his return. The father still sees his son through the eyes of a parent, full of compassion and forgiveness. He isn't judging the mistakes of his son's past; he sees the potential in him.

God is our father. He is patiently waiting for us to come to our senses and return home. He wants to wrap His loving arms around us and let us know how much He loves us and desires a relationship with us. Jesus said in Luke 15:10 there is joy in God's presence when one repents and comes home.

I firmly believe the Gospel offers the one thing for all who suffer from addiction—hope. The Gospel is more than a story of forgiveness. The Gospel offers the redemption and restoration we all long for. It details the story of God, who created all things, suffered the pain of watching His creation become separated from Him through sin, and showcases the great lengths He went through to restore this relationship.

The Gospel offers hope of a new life that we desperately crave and were created for. Life can be different. We don't have to continue to live the same lives we have always lived because of our addictions.

The second reason I wrote this book is to describe how the Gospel meets the deepest needs of men and women who suffer from addiction. The Gospel is the road to the hope and healing that we long for and desperately want to find.

Chapter one examines a few questions: What is addiction? How does it work? How does it affect people?

In chapter two, we take a look at God's love for His creation and us. The foundation of the Gospel is God's love for us and His creation.

In chapter three, we take a look at what it means to be created in God's image, which is the foundation for our value, worth, and dignity. The Gospel holds out hope for restoration of who we are meant to be.

The Gospel also speaks to the brokenness of our world and our relationships. But how did everything become so broken? In chapter four, we examine how this happened and the consequences of sin.

God's remedy to the consequences of sin is found in the Gospel. In chapter five, we look at His solution and how we can take hold of it.

The Gospel promises we won't stay the same after accepting Jesus' forgiveness. In chapter six, we look at some of the most important changes we experience in our new lives.

Chapter seven reveals who is with us on this new journey of life. The Gospel promises we don't have to experience our new life alone.

As you read this book, my prayer is that you will begin to view those who suffer from addiction as men and women who are in need of God's mercy, grace, and hope. I want you to see them as people in need of connection to God, others, and themselves.

I also pray that it might be a source of hope for you. My hope is this book will give you a new understanding of the Gospel. The Gospel delivers good news to those who suffer from addiction and offers the ultimate source of hope. God's view of those who suffer from addiction is not one of judgement and condemnation, but rather one of love and desire for relationship. I hope this book can become a useful tool in sharing the hope we have in Christ. Forgiveness, redemption, and restoration are possible. It's not just a dream; it's for everyone.

Scripture References

Luke 15:11–32
And He said, "A man had two sons. The younger of them said to his father, 'Father, give me the share of the estate that falls to me.' So he divided his wealth between them. "And not many days later, the younger son gathered everything together and went on a journey into a distant country, and there he squandered his estate with loose living. Now when he had spent everything, a severe famine occurred in that country, and he began to be impoverished. So he went and hired himself out to one of the citizens of that country, and he sent him into his fields to feed swine. And he would have gladly filled his stomach with the pods that the swine were eating, and no one was giving *anything* to him. But when he came to his senses, he said, 'How many of my father's hired men have more than enough bread, but I am dying here with hunger! 'I will get up and go to my father, and will say to him, "Father, I have sinned against heaven, and in your sight; I am no longer worthy to be called your son; make me as one of your hired men." ' So he got up and came to his father. But while he was still a

long way off, his father saw him and felt compassion *for him,* and ran and embraced him and kissed him. And the son said to him, 'Father, I have sinned against heaven and in your sight; I am no longer worthy to be called your son.' "But the father said to his slaves, 'Quickly bring out the best robe and put it on him, and put a ring on his hand and sandals on his feet; and bring the fattened calf, kill it, and let us eat and celebrate; for this son of mine was dead and has come to life again; he was lost and has been found.' And they began to celebrate. Now his older son was in the field, and when he came and approached the house, he heard music and dancing. And he summoned one of the servants and *began* inquiring what these things could be. And he said to him, 'Your brother has come, and your father has killed the fattened calf because he has received him back safe and sound.' But he became angry and was not willing to go in; and his father came out and *began* pleading with him. But he answered and said to his father, 'Look! For so many years I have been serving you and I have never neglected a command of yours; and *yet* you have never given me a young goat, so that I might celebrate with my friends; but when this son of yours came, who has devoured your wealth with prostitutes, you killed the fattened calf for him.' And he said to him, 'Son, you have always been with me, and all that is mine is yours. But we had to celebrate and rejoice, for this brother of yours was dead and *has begun* to live, and *was* lost and has been found.'"

Luke 15:10

"In the same way, I tell you, there is joy in the presence of the angels of God over one sinner who repents."

1

WHAT IS ADDICTION?

There are all kinds of addicts, I guess. We all have pain. And we all look for ways to make the pain go away.
—HealthyPlace.com

No one is immune from addiction; it afflicts people of all ages, races, classes, and professions.
—Patrick J. Kennedy

What is addiction? There is no consensus of opinion to answer this question. The following are a few definitions.

The American Psychiatric Association (APA) defines addiction as a "complex condition, a brain disease that is manifested by compulsive substance use despite harmful consequence."[1]

The National Institute on Drug Abuse (NIDA) defines addiction as a "chronic, relapsing disorder characterized by compulsive drug seeking, continued use despite harmful consequences, and long-lasting changes in the brain. It is considered both a complex brain disorder and a mental illness."[2]

The American Society of Addiction Medicine defines addiction as "a primary, chronic disease of brain reward, motivation, memory and related circuitry. Dysfunction in these circuits leads to characteristic biological, psychological, social and spiritual manifestations."[3]

Dr. Kevin McCauley, in his documentary *Pleasure Unwoven*, gives a working definition of addiction. He defines it as "stress induced defect, acting on a genetic vulnerability, in the reward/learning area of the midbrain and the emotional choice area of the frontal cortex."[4]

Gerald May, in his book *Addiction and Grace*, defines addiction as "any compulsive, habitual behavior that limits freedom of human desire."[5]

It's easy to understand why there is no standard definition of addiction. Yet despite the varying definitions, they all have commonalities.

First, all addictions are behaviors; some even describe addiction as a compulsive behavior. When those who suffer from addictions are indulging, they feel compelled to use because the addiction has taken over their lives. They feel they have no choice. They *have* to use. They develop a relationship with their addiction that becomes so strong they can't imagine life without it. They start to crave their addiction.

Second, all addictions have consequences. "Meth mouth," abscesses, infections from shooting up, HIV, and

Hepatitis C are just some of the possible consequences. Loss of employment, jail or prison time, life on parole or probation, and the label of being a felon are not adequate deterrents to keep some from using. Broken relationships, guilt, and shame are consequences that keep people in their addiction. Yet, despite these and other negative consequences, they continue to live in their addiction.

Another consequence is the change in personality, inability to care about others, and the inability to properly care for oneself. Those who suffer from addiction tend to become more irritable, angry, and isolated. Those of us who suffer from addictions tend to only interact with others in order to get our next "fix." Many start to neglect their physical needs. They don't shower or eat properly. Some will urinate or defecate on themselves—unknowingly—when they are passed out. Many don't eat. Many end up homeless after losing everything.

Finally, many people refer to addiction as a disease. Dr. Kevin McCauley describes a disease doing three things: 1) it attacks an organ; 2) it causes damage to an organ; and 3) it causes the symptoms we see and experience. All addictions do the same things: they attack our brains, damage our ability to make decisions, and result in the poor behavior we see in those who suffer from addiction.[6]

How Does Addiction Work?

Dr. Kevin McCauley describes how addiction impacts our brains. He describes five levels of functioning. The first involves our genetic makeup. All of us are genetically vulnerable to becoming addicted to something. For some, it takes a lot of exposure and experience for us to become addicted to something. For others, it doesn't take much for it to happen. Either way, however, this vulnerability isn't enough to cause us to become addicted to something. We must experience something that plays on this vulnerability and leads us toward becoming addicted.

The second way addiction messes with our brains is through how we experience pleasure. We do things because they either bring us pleasure or they don't. All of us have a sense of what makes us feel good, brings enjoyment, makes us happy, and causes us to feel successful.

This pleasure sense is not found in our frontal cortex—the area of the brain where we make choices—but in the midbrain. The midbrain assigns pleasure to our experiences. It sends the message that something is good for us, so we need to remember it in order to do it again. We can get rewarded for "good behavior."

This sense is called our hedonic capacity, or our pleasure sense. This is a natural, or normal, capacity. Things that *should* make us feel good actually *do* make us feel good. For some that might be taking a hike, helping others, or, in my case, birdwatching. What addiction does is take this pleasure sense to a level that is so high, things we used to find pleasure in are no longer pleasurable. The only thing that makes us happy is our addiction.

The third way addiction messes with our brain is in the formation of our memories. The midbrain helps form memories based on whether the experience was pleasurable of not. If the experience was pleasurable, or good, then the midbrain files it away so we can remember it and repeat the activity in order to experience the pleasurable feeling again. If the experience was not pleasurable, then the midbrain records it as a negative experience so we can avoid it in the future. Addiction hijacks this part of the process and makes the experience of using so pleasurable that nothing compares to it. It also tempts us to use so we can avoid negative emotions and memories. Through addiction, we can temporarily avoid feeling bad or reliving bad experiences.

The fourth way addiction negatively affects us is in how we handle stress. We talked about our hedonic capacity. This the set point to which we get pleasure from life's experiences. At times we can get overloaded with pleasurable experiences and experience a "high." We do something for so long that the pleasure overwhelms us. Runners sometimes feel this as a "runner's high." Eventually the brain pushes back against this high, and when we come down our hedonic set point returns to normal.

This is how it should work. We should be able to have pleasurable experiences and be able to live with healthy highs. Addiction, however, screws this up. We were not made to live in a state of feeling high twenty-four hours a day. Addiction provides a pleasurable experience that far exceeds what a normal experience provides. After repeated addiction cycles, the brain can't handle the level of pleasure it is experiencing. So in order to handle this, it raises the hedonic set point. Addiction forces the brain to raise the set point high enough so it can handle the addiction-induced pleasure. Normal activities that used to be pleasurable are no longer pleasurable. The only thing that brings pleasure is the addiction.

Stress is something we all experience. We experience stress at work, at home, at church, and even within ourselves. None of us like stress. It gets our adrenaline going. It adds pressure to a situation that is already hard enough to handle. It can raise expectations to the point that we feel like we can't handle it.

This is where the allure of addictions gets its power. Our addictions say, "Come to me, and I will give you rest. I can take that stress from you, and you don't have to worry about it anymore." The problem is it can't completely deliver its promise. Once the high is gone, the stress is still there. This leads us back to our addiction to find the relief it continues to promise us, which it can't deliver. Soon we get caught up in living in the addiction in order to deal with any stressful situation we experience. We get trapped in a cycle from which there seems to be no way out.

This is why addiction is so hideous. It preys on our genetic vulnerability. It promises to give us a better life and burns this idea into our memories, even when it can't deliver on that promise. Finally, it stresses our brains in ways that makes addiction feel like the only way we can manage all the pressures we face.

There is one more way addiction interferes in our lives. It compromises our ability to make choices. The frontal cortex is where we make choices, develop our morals and spiritual life, and it is where we decide on what's wrong and what's right. It is where we make choices of what we do and how we live.[7]

The frontal cortex normally overrides the midbrain in our decision-making. We are able to assess our thoughts and feelings and decide if we will do something or not. We base these choices on what we think is right or wrong, will we be successful or not, will we hurt others or not, and will we get hurt or not.

Addiction flips this around. When someone is living in their addiction, the midbrain is overriding the frontal cortex. Decisions and choices are now based on what will provide the most pleasure. Our addiction has taken advantage of a genetic vulnerability, made itself the only thing that can provide pleasure, burned this into our memory, and has added enough stress to our lives that only it can relieve. Our addiction becomes the driving force in all our decisions and choices. Because it is the only source of pleasure in our lives, we pursue it with everything we have. Our worlds revolve around it.

This is why many of us who suffer from addictions can't handle stressful situations. This why we can't quit for our loved ones, even though we still love them dearly This explains why someone who faces a court date goes out and uses and never shows up. It explains why those who suffer from addictions can't hold a job or make a relationship last without their addiction.

We now have an understanding of what addiction is and how it works. In my opinion, Dr. Kevin McCauley described addiction best when he said, "addiction is a disease of choice." Addiction attacks the very foundation of how we make decisions and choices just as heart disease attacks the heart or cancer attacks the body. It leaves us enslaved to something that's destructive.

Consequences of Addiction

It's a good thing to have a concise definition of addiction and to know how it works, but that doesn't help us understand what it does. Addiction impacts more than just the person suffering from the addiction. Many of us know someone suffering from an addiction or someone whose life has been impacted by it. You may even be a person suffering from an addiction.

I see the impact of addiction every day in the lives of the clients I work with as an addiction counselor. Many of them come in wanting to quit, but they don't believe they can. Their addiction is so strong they don't see any way out. Many have been using for forty to fifty years. Their addictions have become so much a part of their lives, they can't see living without them.

I also get phone calls from family members who want to know how to get their loved one into detox. Many of them relate that they don't know what else to do. Some tell me they are down to their last option to get their loved one help. Many tell me they can't take it anymore.

Addiction changes the way people think. Life becomes all about us. It changes the way we view others. We don't see people; instead, we see objects to be used to get what we want, when we want it, where we want it, and how we want it.

I have seen the impact my own addictions have had in my life. Never feeling good enough, I lived far below my abilities because of shame. I believed from an early age that being smart wasn't a good thing. Instead of using the gifts God gave me, I simply skated by, doing the least amount of work I could, mentally and physically. I became addicted to a lifestyle of not being good enough because I didn't think I was.

I was sexually abused as a child, and this added to the negative way I looked at myself. It also left me vulnerable to pornography, which I was introduced to in fifth grade. My addiction to pornography hit full force in seventh grade. It changed the way I looked at females and the way I looked at life and myself.

I share my struggles because, for most us effected by addiction, there seems to be no hope of overcoming it. I want to share that there is hope to overcome our addictions, however. I have found hope in the Gospel of Jesus Christ. I have found the Gospel can meet our deepest needs and give us a sense of worth, value, and dignity that we can't find anywhere else.

How does it do that? That's what the rest of this book is all about. The Gospel has the answers to our deepest needs. Read on and find out how.

2

GOD STILL LOVES THE MESS WE'RE IN

God's love for us is proclaimed by each sunrise.
—Anonymous

Though our feelings come and go, God's love for us does not.
—C.S. Lewis

Today's world is a real mess. When I look at the political unrest, financial instability, and swiftly changing social picture, I can't help but think about the mess we live in. To be fair, there are two ways to look at our current situation. Some see the problems and are optimistic that we can overcome them. Others look at our current situation and wonder if there is any hope for our future. I tend to go back and forth between these two views.

What both views have in common is the awareness that

there are problems. Political unrest causes us to balance on a precipice between war and peace. The unrest in our global financial market keeps us on the edge of a global recession and possible depression. Society's changing values leave us wondering what's right and what's wrong.

There are other issues too. Natural disasters ravage communities and kill many people. Gun violence and mass shootings are occurring more frequently, and no one seems to know why. Racism and discrimination are ever present. Abuse, whether sexual, physical, verbal, or emotional, is common to all and making headlines daily. Addictions are rampant, with no decline in sight.

Widespread health issues have also come to the forefront. As a culture, we are dealing with obesity, diseases, epidemics, and rising healthcare costs. Diseases such as Alzheimer's and dementia are particularly ravaging because they place huge emotional, physical, and financial stress on family members that are seeking to provide the best care for their loved ones while also managing their own lives.

Society's standards seem to be changing daily. The right thing to do today is wrong tomorrow. Advertisers prey on our insecurities. We have to wear the right clothes and drive the right cars or we don't meet society's standards of acceptance. Even these standards seem to change every day. There seems to be no consistency, no solid footing, for us to base our lives on.

The church is not exempt from these issues. Local churches and denominations split over issues of doctrine. Division seems to be the standard instead of unity. In many circles the church seems to be the problem—not the solution.

I can feel the fear that permeates our world. It brings

with it an uncertainty about our future—globally, nationally, and locally. Often I feel out of control and powerless over my life, as do many others. Our relationships suffer because we can't trust others for fear they might take advantage of us or abuse us. The world is no longer a safe place.

Anxiety comes at us from all directions as we worry about our future. Do we have what it takes to survive? Can we provide for our families? Will our basic needs (food, shelter, and clothing) be met? Will our relationships be what we desire, or are we destined to be alone in this life?

Love has become nothing more than a feeling. Commitment no longer means anything in our relationships. If we "don't feel it" or we "fall out of love," we move on to the next relationship. Life becomes an empty shell without any meaning or foundation.

Life is messy. It can lead to happiness, but more often than not, it leads to an emptiness that leads to pain and heartache. I learned early in life that no one was there for me. Many multiple overnight stays in the hospital as a very young child taught me this. I felt different and alone due to limitations relating to my asthma. I couldn't play the way other kids did. I felt like the odd man out in school, at church, and even at home. I was bullied, harassed, and ridiculed. I grew up thinking and feeling that I was never going to be good enough for anyone or anything—even God.

My life was a web of codependent relationships that always fell apart quickly. This just fueled my belief that I deserved to be alone. My journey into addiction to fear, pornography, and people pleasing was fueled by this, and it deepened by the day.

I hear the same story from my clients. Many talk of

growing up in families where they were invisible or where they were beaten or abused. Some grew up in families with drug users or alcoholics. For many, this was a normal way of life.

Others, like myself, were sexually abused, physically abused, verbally, and/or emotionally abused. We learn early on that trust was not something to be given lightly. We couldn't trust anyone not to hurt us. Relationships were shallow or nonexistent.

Some grew up in families where they felt pressure to perform. They were told, "You can do better," as if what they had accomplished didn't matter. Many of my clients felt like they could never measure up.

As a licensed addiction counselor and licensed professional counselor, I see the impact living in this world has on the lives of people. I see the scars of the hurt and pain caused by years of feeling abandoned and alone. The loss and destruction of innocence and life through all types of abuse is evident. There is a devaluing of people simply because they can't seem to measure up to society's standards.

I think the question we need to ask isn't why people suffer from addiction, but why don't more suffer from it? My point is that we live in a screwed up world. We experience so many things I don't think God ever intended for us to experience. Yet, here we are in a mess of our own doing. We've screwed it up so much, at times, I think we are justified in asking if God does still care about this world. I just wonder if we can handle the answer.

How did our world, and our lives, become so distorted from what God originally intended? Addictions saturate our world. So how did we, as a society, get here? Is this the kind of world we really want to live in? Is it the kind of world we were created to live in? This world seems to be in such a mess, is there any hope for it to be fixed?

Does God really care about us? Do we really matter to Him? Have we screwed up our lives so badly that even He has given up on us? God is supposed to be a God of love, so where is He in this mess?

I have asked these questions many times. It's no surprise to me that many of my clients ask them as well. My guess is that you, the reader, have asked the same questions yourself. We live in a world where it seems He just doesn't care. We see all the pain, hurt, uncertainty, injustice, and abuse, and it begs the question: Where is He? He's supposed to be all-powerful, present everywhere, all-knowing, and all loving, so why doesn't He stop all this destruction and rescue us? Inquiring minds want to know.

I've come to realize these answers are crucial to helping us overcome our addictions. We need to know God offers the hope of restoration and redemption we long for. We need to know He is there and still cares. The Gospel is God's powerful answer to these questions with an affirmative YES! God does care, and He hasn't given up on us. He remains present here in this mess, even if we can't see Him.

One thing that God has shown me through the Gospel, however, is He was always there, always loved me, and always wanted me. I may not have felt it, but God's desire for a relationship with me was not based on how I performed; it's always been about what He has done. As we will see, God is continuing to teach me that His love for me is not based on what I do or what's been done to me. His love is steadfast simply because He created me in His image. This is true for everyone.

God Does Care About His Creation

I think we must look at why God *would* care about His creation in order to understand that He *does* care about it. We need to go back to the beginning in Genesis 1 to start this journey.

Just a note as we begin here. There are different views on the creation story. Some take it literally as being done in six days. Some think it was done over a period of time, not a literal six days. Others will look at it as a type of creation literature, that it was written in the style of creation literature of the time. I am taking the position that what was written was exactly what God wants us to know about creation. God created it. So for the purposes of this book that is my focus.

Genesis 1:1 states, "In the beginning God created the heavens and the earth." God created this planet that we live on. He created the heavens, the oceans, the continents, and everything found in them. This is important for several reasons.

First, God was deliberate in making it. God chose to make it. His creation was thoughtful and intentional.

Second, planning and time went into making His creation. Genesis 1 and 2 show that creation was created in stages. Each stage builds on the previous one.

Third, God cared about what He created. After each stage, the Book of Genesis states that God saw everything as good and then very good after He created Adam and Eve. Clearly, God had a stake in what He created; therefore He had to care about His creation.

God Loves His Creation

If God cares so much about His creation, then why has He allowed us to screw it up so badly? Just because we've screwed it up doesn't mean God doesn't care about and love His creation.

Ask yourself a question. If you have kids, grandkids, nieces, or nephews, do you stop loving them just because they screw things up? No, they are your family. You still love them, though you may not like what they're doing or have done. If you plant a garden or create a project and it gets messed up, do you get angry? Yes, because you care about what you created. You care because what you created is no longer how you created it; yet the love you put into it does not go away just because it has been messed up.

You love it no matter what. And because you love it, your desire is for it to be restored to the way it was before it was screwed up. There is a longing for restoration and redemption of relationship. It is the same with God, only His love for His creation goes deeper than ours ever could.

John states it the best in John 3:16–17 when he wrote: "For God so loved the world, that He gave His only begotten Son, that whoever believes in Him shall not perish, but have eternal life. For God did not send the Son into the world to judge the world, but that the world might be saved through Him."

Paul echoes this in Romans 8:20–22: "For the creation was subjected to futility, not willingly, but because of Him who subjected it, in hope that the creation itself also will be set free from its slavery to corruption into the freedom of the glory of the children of God. For we know that the whole creation groans and suffers the pains of childbirth together until now."

A couple of observations stand out to me from these passages. First, God loves his creation, even if we have screwed it up. God doesn't condemn the world; instead He wants to save it. Second, God's desire is to redeem and restore creation to what it was meant to be—free from corruption. God has never stopped loving His creation.

It is hard to understand this kind of unconditional love. I, like my clients, have a hard time accepting this to be true. It's hard to reconcile this kind of love with the current state of the world. It's a mess. I think most of those who suffer from addictions have a hard time reconciling this, as do those whose lives are impacted by their loved one's or friend's addictions. Why it is so important that we understand this?

It is important because we are the final and greatest piece of His creation. Only people are created in His image. Genesis 1:26–27 clarifies this: "Then God said, "Let Us make man in Our image, according to Our likeness. . . . God created man in His own image, in the image of God He created him; male and female He created them." God stated that after He created the plants and animals, what He created was *good*. It wasn't until He created Adam and Eve that He said His creation was *very good*.

It is the fact that we are made in His image that sets us apart from the rest of creation. We all have intrinsic value, worth, and dignity simply because we live. God has given it to us, not because of what we do or don't do, but because He has chosen to give it to us by creating us in His image. This is why He loves us and the rest of creation, even though we have screwed all of it up.

David wrote about this in Psalm 8:3–5: "When I consider Your heavens, the work of Your fingers, the moon and the stars, which You have ordained; what is man that

You take thought of him, and the son of man that You care for him? Yet You have made him a little lower than God, And You crown him with glory and majesty!" This includes all of us, even those who suffer from addictions and their family and friends.

Even today, I still have a hard time understanding this kind of love. Though we have messed up our lives, shattered relationships with family and friends, and become slaves to our addictions, all of us are still created in God's image. Although we have screwed up our lives and this world and deeply hurt and angered Him, God still loves us simply because He has created us in His image.

So what does it mean to be made in God's image? We'll take a look at this in the next chapter. In the meantime, here are some questions to consider:

1. What keeps you from believing God is present in this world?
2. What keeps you from believing that God still loves this world?
3. What keeps you from believing God loves you?
4. What keeps you from seeing how He is working in your life?
5. What hinders you from seeing that God loves those who suffer from addictions?

Scripture References

Genesis 1:1

"In the beginning God created the heavens and the earth."

John 3:16–17

"For God so loved the world, that He gave His only begotten Son, that whoever believes in Him shall not perish, but have eternal life. For God did not send the Son into the world to judge the world, but that the world might be saved through Him."

Romans 8:20–21

"For the creation was subjected to futility, not willingly, but because of Him who subjected it, in hope that the creation itself also will be set free from its slavery to corruption into the freedom of the glory of the children of God."

Genesis 1:26–27

"Then God said, 'Let Us make man in Our image, according to Our likeness; and let them rule over the fish of the sea and over the birds of the sky and over the cattle and over all the earth, and over every creeping thing that creeps on the earth.' God created man in His own image, in the image of God He created him; male and female He created them."

Psalm 8:3–5
"When I consider Your heavens, the work of Your
 fingers,
The moon and the stars, which You have ordained;
What is man that You take thought of him,
And the son of man that You care for him?
Yet You have made him a little lower than God,
And You crown him with glory and majesty!"

3

WE ARE CREATED IN GOD'S IMAGE

Within each of us exists the image of God, however disfigured and corrupted by sin it may presently be. God is able to recover this image through grace as we are conformed to Christ.
—Alister McGrath

The great God of the universe who heaped up the mountains, scooped out the oceans, and flung out the stars wants to have a relationship with you.
—Adrian Rogers

In the last chapter, we established that God does, in fact, still love this world even though we've made a mess of it. Most important, I offered that He still loves us, not for what we have or haven't done, but because He created us in His image.

Being created in the image of God can be difficult to understand. What does the image of God mean? Does God look like us? Do we look like Him?

I must admit it has taken me years to start to understand what it means to be created in God's image. Over time, I came to appreciate the importance of this truth because it is at the core of who we are. It is statement about our worth, value, and dignity. It is a solid foundation for our lives that won't crumble under the weight of everyday life. It is why God wants a relationship with us and was willing to die to restore and redeem it.

I think the Bible is clear we are made in God's image. We aren't God, but as Larry Crabb explains in his book *Understanding People*, we are created as "image-bearers." Crabb goes on to describe how we bear God's image in four ways; as image-bearers we think, we feel, we make choices, and we live in relationship to the world around us.[1]

Created in God's Image: We Can Think

The Bible is full of God's thoughts about His creation, about us, about how we are separated from Him, and how He wants to restore and redeem us and His creation. The Bible gives us a glimpse into His plans for the redemption and restoration of His relationship with us. It gives us a picture of how important to Him we really are.

God has given us this ability to think as part of being created in His image. The problem is—as created creatures —our ability to think is not as perfect as God ability. Isaiah 55:9 states that our thoughts are not the same as God's. This is true, because we can't see things from his perspective; we don't know what will happen in the future as He does. His thoughts are based on eternity; ours are based in fixed time and space.

Yet, we still make judgements, decisions, plans, and build our beliefs on what we think. I think this begs the questions: What will we build our thoughts on? What do we build our belief system on? Do we build them on what is true, or do we build our thoughts and beliefs on lies?

Created in God's Image: We Can Feel

God shows a full range of emotions throughout the Bible. God shows joy, love, acceptance, and patience. God also shows anger, frustration, hurt, and sadness. Through Jesus, He shared in our pain. He knows what it is to feel rejected, abandoned, betrayed, and long for relationship with us and His creation as Matthew 23:37 shows.

We are able to experience a full range of emotions because we are created in His image. We all know what it is to feel excited, loved, wanted, accepted, and significant. We also know what it means to feel abandoned, hurt, sad, betrayed, unloved, and unaccepted. I suspect many feel abandoned, hurt, sad, betrayed, unloved, and unaccepted more often than we feel excited, loved, wanted, accepted, and significant. This is why addiction has come to have a foothold in so many peoples' lives.

Created in God's Image: We Make Choices

God demonstrates how He makes choices throughout Scripture. God chooses to still love us even though we've screwed it up. God has judged sin and paid the price for it (more on this later). God chose to make a way for us to be redeemed and restored to relationship with Him, others, and ourselves.

We are able to make choices because we are made in God's image. Our choices in life are made off the judgements, decisions, plans, and beliefs we base our lives on. We go here, we go there. Take this job; quit that job. We decide what to wear or not wear. When to use or not to use.

We also make moral choices. We are able to choose between love and hate. We can decide to treat people with the honor, dignity, and respect due them because they are made in God's image, or we can use and abuse them. We can choose to look out for the needs of others, or we can choose to be self-centered and ignore them.

We should ask ourselves, What choices are we making, and what are these choices based on?

Created in God's Image: We Are Made to Live in Relationship

Living in relationship is at the heart of who God is—God the Father, God the Son, and God the Holy Spirit. In my opinion, the fact that God is relational is at the heart of why He created us in His image. He desires to have relationship with us.

This is demonstrated throughout the Old Testament as God continually calls to Israel to come back to Him and why He unceasingly woos her back to Him. It is shown in the New Testament when God chooses to make the ultimate sacrifice to make it possible for us to be in relationship with Him.

Likewise, we were made to live in relationship with each other. Making friends and finding romantic partners is high on our list of things to do. Building family and community are important. If we are honest, all of this isn't easy. In fact, most of us need improvement in this area of our lives.

Finally, we live in relationship with ourselves. We all know what that's like—hard. Very few of us really like ourselves as we are. We are always looking for ways to improve ourselves, to become more acceptable to others and ourselves.

All of us have descriptive words we use when we do something wrong or we're not successful: stupid, idiot, failure. We all have them and use them without mercy because we know something's wrong and we can't identify it.

Yes, living in relationship is hard. Yet we were made for relationship, and our lives are empty without it. We are not made to live in isolation. This is why many choose to live in relationship with their addiction when times get tough. Sometimes it feels easier to live with an addiction than it is being in relationship with people.

Those who suffer from addictions are made in God's image.

All of us are made God's image, even those who suffer from addictions. God didn't make a distinction for those who suffer from addictions. Nor did God make a distinction for those who are not Jewish or Christians. Everyone is created in His image.

I want to make two statements here before we go on. First, those who suffer from addictions still think. We still feel. We make choices. We live in relationship whether we like it or not. We bear the image of God.

Second, it is my belief that all people have at least one addiction. Our addictions take on a variety of activities. Some are socially acceptable, others are not. Some are more destructive than others. Some, like me, have more than one.

No matter what our addiction is, we use it to live life without God. We try to control and exercise power over everything and everyone. We can't handle being out of control or powerless, so we turn to our addiction to numb to the pain we experience when feeling out of control and powerless.

My challenge to you, the reader, is to ask yourself, "Do I see myself in this chapter?" If you have the courage, I encourage you to ask what David did of God in Psalm 139:23–24 when he wrote, "Search me, God, and know my heart; test me and know my concerns. See if there is any offensive way in me; lead me in the everlasting way."

We Think

My favorite verse comes from Proverbs 23:7: "For as he thinks within himself, so he is." What we think about ourselves, others, and God is critical to how we live. It helps form the foundation for the beliefs we hold on to in order to live our lives.

Our thoughts and beliefs act as a filter, or framework, that we look at life through. This filter is based on our life experiences, both good and bad. We use this filter to make decisions, form judgements about people, places, and things, and to plan our lives accordingly. It helps us set our expectations of ourselves, others, and God.

We automatically dismiss something as not true if

something doesn't fit through our filter or threatens our belief framework. Often we twist something to make it fit what we believe. We do whatever it takes to protect our filters because they're how we make sense out of life.

The best way to demonstrate this is to look at how we deal with compliments. Do you accept a compliment at face value, or is there a slight twinge because you don't really believe it? Do you think to yourself, *If they only knew they wouldn't say that*. Or, *I'm nothing special*? Do you get embarrassed when people compliment you? The answers to these questions all indicate what we think of ourselves.

Addiction is a lifestyle we choose to live. This lifestyle is built on a set of core beliefs and thoughts we have about ourselves, others, and God. What are some of the core beliefs and thoughts you have?

First, we can't stand ourselves because of our addictions. We look at what we do and ask why? We don't understand why our addiction is so important to us. Sometimes it seems to help us through stressful times. It provides an escape from reality where we feel free from the world. We know, however, that when we sober up, the stress and problems are still there, waiting for us.

This continuous running back to our addiction leaves us thinking we are weak, which adds to our feelings of guilt and shame. We start to hate how we are living and what we see ourselves becoming. Yet this just drives us deeper into our addiction to escape these feelings and it just becomes a downward spiral with no apparent escape.

We start to think of ourselves not as men and women whom God created, but as those who suffer from addictions who happen to be men and women. We begin to think we are completely powerless and under the control of our addiction. We begin to think we have no choice, that we *have to* live in our addiction. How we think about ourselves really does matter.

We can't stand the fact that we think we can't live up to the expectations of our family and friends. We just can't seem to quit. Even going into rehab and treatment doesn't always work. When we leave, we often relapse immediately. We can't figure out what's wrong with us. We think we're hopeless and useless.

Second, we can't stand how we've hurt everyone who cares about us. We still make promises to quit, yet we don't. We steal from you and lie to your face. We use you to get what we want—often that's a place to stay—if we can. When that doesn't work, we stay on streets and cause you to worry about if we are okay, or even still alive. Though we get angry and tell you to get out of our lives, we want you to know we appreciate your caring for us. We really do love you, we just don't think we can let go of our addictions to show it.

Third, we see ourselves as worthless. We can't see we have something to offer to you or society. We think we have no value to anyone except our dealers and others who choose to live in their addictions. The old saying "misery loves company" is true, and we find a lot of it. We've lost all self-respect and any dignity we had. We don't think we can do anything right except live in our addiction. At least our addiction doesn't judge us and accepts us for who we think we are.

The world isn't a safe place for us. We feel our only purpose in life is to be used, abused, hurt, and abandoned. We don't think we're loved or wanted. We definitely don't think we have what it takes to succeed in life on life's terms.

We think, *Why change? Who's gonna care if we do?* We believe we've burned all our bridges. There's nothing to go back to. We'd be stuck somewhere, sober, and still not know how to deal with life. More thoughts fill our chaotic mind: *God cares? Who is God? Isn't He just a higher power of my own understanding? I just can't believe He cares. Why did God allow all the crap to happen to me? Why didn't He stop it?*

Then there's how families and friends respond. Remember, they have a filter as well.

- Why couldn't we see this happening?
- How did we miss the signs?
- We thought we knew our loved one better than this.
- We hoped that they would come talk to us, or someone else, when things got bad.
- We thought they knew we loved them.
- What could we have done different to stop this from happening?
- Now that it's happened, what do we do next?
- How can we help our friend or loved one sober up and quit?

In addition, many want to know if their loved one cares about them:

- They say they love us, but their actions are definitely not showing this.
- Do they really care about us? Obviously, they don't care what they do to us because they just keep on living in their addiction.

- We wish they would turn their lives around because we still love them, but it's hard to keep loving them when they show no desire to quit.
- We're losing hope that they will ever turn around and come back to us.
- Are we destined to watch our loved one die from their addiction, knowing there's nothing we can do to stop it?

Many who suffer from addictions —as well as friends and family members—ask the question: Where is God in all of this mess? They pray and nothing seems to happen. God seems to be silent in the midst of their pain and heartache. They begin to think that God has abandoned them in their darkest moment.

These are just some of the thoughts I hear coming from my clients. Many of them feel hopeless, unwanted, and alone. Those who live on the streets tell me story after story of how it's not safe for them. Many are robbed or beaten up for a backpack or a coat. Many have resigned themselves to this lifestyle because they see no hope for getting out of it.

I related to this way of thinking in my own life when I was caught in the grips of addiction. I couldn't stand myself for many years. I lived in fear of being exposed as the fraud I thought I was. I can count at least seven times I thought about killing myself, but I didn't because I couldn't figure out how make it look like an accident.

I thought I didn't have anything to offer and was scared of entering into a real relationship with a woman. So I got into pornography, which worked for a while. After all, a picture wouldn't expect or ask anything of me. It was safe. It didn't last long though.

I couldn't figure out where God was in this mess. Though I grew up in the church and sang in the youth choir, I felt like an outsider. I never thought I fit in with the other kids at church.

Our thoughts are powerful. Proverbs 18:20–21 says that our words have the ability to kill someone or to bring them life. If our words and thoughts are always destructive, how can we expect to live anything different in our relationships?

We Feel

Those who suffer from addictions are no different than anyone else. We, too, have feelings. Most of the time we express our emotions in anger. Our anger is often focused on others and a system that sets us up for failure. Mostly it's aimed at ourselves.

We live in a society that feeds into our belief that we aren't good enough and that we are worthless. Our entire advertising system is predicated and dedicated to awakening these thoughts and emotions within us. You gotta have the right car, go to the right party, shop at the right store. It goes on and on. When we think who we are is based on who society tells us we are, we will lose every time.

Anger isn't the only emotion we feel. We know how to feel happy, joyful, wanted, accepted, and not alone when we relate with those who have the same, or similar, addiction. We also feel these emotions when we are in the midst of acting out in our addiction. These emotions change when we stop acting out and come down from the high or get sober.

Many of us who suffer from addictions start to feel mostly negative emotions. We judge ourselves more harshly than anyone else. We get angry with ourselves or become complacent. Often we become so numb that we don't care what happens to us anymore. Some go through such bad withdrawals if feels like we're going to die.

We start to embrace a reality that we aren't wanted, loved, accepted, and we are completely alone. The belief that no one cares and that everyone would be better off without us invades our thoughts. Feelings of abandonment and betrayal start to set in. Anxiety, paranoia, depression, and a sense of apathy anchors in our psyche. We lose hope for a better life. Suicide becomes an option for some.

Finally, we feel the hardest emotions of all: guilt and shame. We feel the guilt because we know what we've done. We know who we've hurt and who we've let down. We start to feel the shame because we judge ourselves and feel the judgement of others. We see these emotions as the final words on our lives, with no hope for redemption.

Family members and friends experience a range of emotions. One emotion is anger. Anger at their loved ones for destroying their lives. Anger for having to watch this happen and not be able to do anything about. For some, this anger gets to the point that they wash their hands of the loved one and cut them off. This anger ruins the lives of the family member and the loved one.

Others feel anger toward themselves. They deeply feel the sadness, disappointment, and hurt as they watch the loved one destroy themself. They ask, "What could I have done different?" Many will start to enable the loved one in their addiction to ease their sadness, disappointment, and hurt.

Many family members and friends will feel guilt and shame around the anger. Guilt comes from the family member and friend feeling like they didn't do enough. The feeling is that they could have done more or paid closer attention so they didn't miss the signs of the loved one's behaviors.

Shame sets in because they feel the judgement of themselves, others, and society in general. How could they let their family member end up in their addiction? Many parents feel the judgment of others with questions like, "How could you raise such a child? It's all your fault your child is an addict." The embarrassment becomes unbearable at times. Many lose hope that change is possible.

We Make Choices

We make choices all the time. Our choices are influenced by our experiences and our thoughts, beliefs, and feelings about those experiences. For example, experiences that lead us to success or that cause us to feel good are experiences we will want to repeat. On the other hand, if an experience brings us pain, hurt, or abuse, then we won't want to repeat it.

Making choices is easy for those of us living in our addictions. We will always choose anything that helps us to pursue our addictions. We become self-absorbed with it. We can't live without it. Our world revolves around it.

Everything we do—our experiences, thoughts, beliefs, and feelings—revolves around us. We are the most important person in our lives. We expect everyone else to see things the same way. If we say we need it, then everyone is supposed to drop everything and make sure we get it.

When this doesn't work, which is most of the time, we make other choices. We lie, steal, and cheat to get what we want. It doesn't matter who we use or hurt, including ourselves. It doesn't matter if we face jail or prison time. It doesn't matter that we may put ourselves in physical danger. It only matters that we get what we want.

Continuing in this lifestyle is an easy choice for those of us who choose to continue to live in addiction. Many of us think, believe, and feel we are useless. It's easy to believe we have no value or worth. Our experiences help us to hold onto the belief that we are alone, that no cares about us, and that we've been abandoned. We're only good for being used, abused, hurt, and forgotten. Why not seek refuge and relief from the pain, hurt, and loneliness we experience by living in our addictions?

Our family and friends face a different set of choices. They must choose how they want to relate to us. Some may never want to see us again and disown us. Some may choose to enable us because of their own guilt. Still others will take a "tough love" stance and demand we change. There will be consequences if we don't change.

Our family and friends still love us but wonder if they are strong enough to hang in there when we make life tough for them? How do they hold on to us when we keep pushing them away? How will they continue to live with the hurt, pain, and disappointment they experience at our hands? Will they run from us because it becomes too hard to stay engaged? Can they be patient with us as we try to decide if we want to quit? Can they stay with us through multiple relapses on the way out of our addictions?

In some ways our family and friends have it harder

than we do. We at least have an idea of what we want to do and where our lives are headed. Our family and friends have no clue. Many live not knowing if we are still alive, hurt, or if they will get the phone call telling them we're dead. They live with the uncertainty of how we are doing.

We Live in Relationship

God has created us to live in relationship with Him, with others, and with ourselves. Yet relationships can be hard. Relationships with other people require risk and a level of vulnerability that scares the crap out of us. Conversely, relationship with our addictions don't feel risky—or so we think.

Relationships can be scary for a lot of reasons. Being in a relationship with someone gives them a level of power in our lives. The deeper the relationship, the more power I give you to either hurt me or support me in some way. The deeper the relationship, the more I open myself up to being judged by you.

We risk people seeing parts of us we don't want them to see. We fear exposure of the skeletons in our closets believing, if others saw them, they would run from us. You might not like what you see or find in me. I open myself up to feeling guilt and shame at a deep level. So we put up walls and wear masks. We set limits to how far we will let people into our lives.

Those of us who live in our addictions find relationships with people particularly hard. We find it hard to trust that others have our best interests at heart. We've been hurt, abused, used, and mistreated enough that we don't trust many people.

Others who suffer from more socially acceptable addictions find it hard to trust too. What happens if my addiction becomes exposed? How will people look at me? Will they judge me? What happens to me when the facade I've put up comes crashing down?

It is often easier to build a relationship with our addiction than it is with people. Our addiction doesn't judge us. It accepts us as we are. It will always be there, waiting with open arms. It won't reject us. It promises relief from the problems of life and fellowship with others who suffer from the same or similar issues.

Addiction does deliver on these promises. It doesn't, however, tell us that it will cost us everything. We will damage or lose all of our relationships with our loved ones, friends, and ourselves. We will settle for a life we were never meant to settle for.

To summarize, then, those of us who suffer from addiction are made in God's image. We do think, feel, make choices, and live in relationship; but we don't do it in the way we were intended to in the Garden of Eden. Instead of using our ability to think, feel, and make choices that enable us to build a relationship with God, we run and hide from Him. We use these abilities to tear our relationships down instead of building them up.

What happened to us? How did the image of God in us become so distorted and damaged that we actually use it to run and hide from God? How is it that we have become so afraid of finding intimacy that we put up walls and keep each other from seeing who we really are? We'll take a look at these questions and try to answer them in the next chapter.

Consider

1. What do you think it means to be created in the image of God?
2. Does understanding that those of us who suffer from addiction are created in God's image change the way you see us?
3. Addictions can be more than just drugs and alcohol. What things in your life do you see yourself possibly addicted to?

Scripture References

Matthew 23

"Jerusalem, Jerusalem, who kills the prophets and stones those who are sent to her! How often I wanted to gather your children together, the way a hen gathers her chicks under her wings, and you were unwilling."

Psalm 139:23–24

"Search me, O God, and know my heart; Try me and know my anxious thoughts; And see if there be any hurtful way in me, And lead me in the everlasting way."

Proverbs 23:7

"For as he thinks within himself, so he is. He says to you, 'Eat and drink!' But his heart is not with you."

Proverbs 18:20–21

"With the fruit of a man's mouth his stomach will be satisfied;
He will be satisfied with the product of his lips.
Death and life are in the power of the tongue,
And those who love it will eat its fruit."

4

OUR WORLD IS BROKEN

Sin has many tools, but a lie is the handle that fits them all.
—Anonymous

Brokenness is the operative issue of our time - broken souls, broken hearts, broken places.
—Samantha Power

Have you ever been in a place that you thought was absolutely perfect? Life can't get any better than when you were there? For me that place is Pt. Pelee in Canada. Pt. Pelee is one of the best places in North America to go birdwatching in the spring. Seeing the birds and hearing the waves on the lake gently breaking on the shoreline is one of the most relaxing things I have experienced.

I believe that is what the Garden of Eden was for Adam and Eve. Genesis tells us that life in the Garden was perfect. God created the earth, then He created man and woman and said it was very good. I believe it was perfect because there was no sin. There was no discrimination, no racism, no natural disasters, no disease, no war, and no greed in the Garden. There was perfect intimacy between Adam and Eve and between them and God.

We leave these "perfect places" and come back to a world that isn't perfect. We suffer from wars or threats of wars instead of peace. It's filled with inequality instead of equality. Discrimination and racism of all types exist. Natural disasters are occurring with greater frequency, bringing with it damage to property and loss of life. People, especially children, are abused, used, and sold into human trafficking instead of being treated with worth, value, dignity, and cherished for who they are. Addiction is rampant. People are feeling helpless and hopeless in the face of what's going on in our world today.

It's clear to me that this world is broken. It's not what it was created to be. There is too much pain, heartache, hurt, and suffering for this world to be what God called very good. Paul gives us a picture of this when he writes in Romans 8:20–21 that creation itself groans and waits for its own redemption.

Sin Broke Everything

How did this world become broken? What changed it from a paradise to a place of pain and suffering? How do we address this problem to fix it? Can we fix this problem? I think to answer these questions we have to go back to the beginning when it all happened.

Adam and Eve had it all in the beginning. They had perfect relationship with God, perfect relationship with His creation, perfect relationship with each other, and a perfect relationship with self. What more could they want or need? All was good until the serpent awakened a desire to be like God within them. They ate the fruit, and all hell literally broke loose. Sin was set loose in the world.

What is sin? Sin is defined in many ways. Some think of sin as "missing the mark", others say to sin means "to break God's Law." Yet, while a good working definition of sin proves helpful, I think we miss the point if we only focus on defining sin. We must focus on what sin has done and face the consequences of sin. No matter how we define sin, I believe sin produces only one outcome: Sin breaks things. Sin broke our relationship with God, with His creation, with others, and ourselves. Sin distorted and damaged the image of God within us.

Our Relationship with God Is Broken

Sin broke our relationship with God. Sin separates us from God. The Bible teaches that God can't tolerate sin in His presence, as stated in Psalm 5:4–5 and 26:4–5. Habakkuk 1:13 states that God can't even look at sin. Sin created a barrier between us and God we can't break down on our own.

Losing our relationship with God brought other consequences. It created a virtual hole inside all of us. This hole leaves all of us with a feeling of emptiness that can't be fully described. We feel a sense of loss of worth, value, dignity, and purpose. We have a hard time making sense of this loss. We try to fill this emptiness with things like success, accomplishments, sex, and relationships—but nothing works. The emptiness always remains.

This emptiness has brought with it a lack of purpose to our lives. God created us to live in relationship with Him. Our purpose was to live in relationship with God and to take care of the world He created.

I am amazed when I think about this. God, the Creator of the universe, created Adam and Eve to live in relationship with Him and to take care of what He created. God could've taken care of the earth by Himself, but instead He entrusted Adam and Eve as His representatives, His image bearers, to do it for Him. They ate the fruit and all of this was lost.

So when we feel we have no purpose in life, we relentlessly seek it by acquiring successful careers, families, and other meaningful relationships. Some try to recapture our original purpose of caring of the earth. We are ultimately left feeling empty and lonely.

This hole has created a need within us to perform. We believe if we are good enough, do the right things, put others first, and live as basically good people, then God will have to love and accept us. Isaiah 64:6 says otherwise though. It states that all of our "good deeds" are like filthy rags before God. Everything we do has been stained by sin and is therefore unacceptable to Him.

Fear and anxiety have become common emotions for all of us. Not only do we feel like we have to perform, but we worry we aren't good enough. Many see God as an overbearing boss, waiting to punish us if we screw up.

This emptiness, feeling like we have to perform, living in fear and anxiety, and not wanting to fail make for fertile soil for addictions. Our addictions become a way to numb the feelings of emptiness and not feeling good enough.

Addiction helps us calm our hearts and souls, if only for a moment. Addiction gives us a sense of control and being powerful that helps relieve our fears and anxieties. But it never lasts. These feelings always come back.

There seems to be no hope it will ever be fixed. The hole will always be there. The emptiness, pain, and suffering we experience will never end.

Addiction Makes Sense

No wonder addiction is a common response. Addiction tells us that if we indulge in it, we won't have to *worry* about being good enough, because we *will* be. Addiction promises "Come as you are, and I'll take away your worries, fears, and anxieties." It makes us believe that it can fill that empty spot inside us.

Eventually, it turns the tables on us. We become not good enough *because* of it. We start to experience the worries, fears, and anxieties it promised to remove. Because when we stop indulging, they are still there.

In fact, our addictions only add to our worries, fears, and anxieties. We worry about getting exposed. We fear others judging us because of our addictions. Anxiety starts to control our lives, and paranoia soon runs rampant.

Personally, I've struggled with these feelings and thoughts about God for a long time. I'm not what I want to be, which is a blameless and sinless image-bearer, living in perfect relationship with God. Instead, I've learned how far I am from this. Many times, I considered killing myself because I felt I couldn't measure up to what God, others, and this world wanted from me.

Even though I've been a Christian for forty years, I've felt like I still had to appease God so He would love me and take care of me. I've learned, however, this isn't true. A better understanding of the Gospel, and what it really says about God and me, has helped me to start to overcome this fear and the anxiety of not being good enough. This truth has begun to fill the emptiness inside of me.

Our Relationships with Others Are Broken

Genesis 2:25 talks about Adam and Eve's relationship. It states that they were "naked and unashamed." They had perfect intimacy with other. They had nothing to hide. They had what we all long for: a perfect relationship without guilt, shame, and conflict.

What a difference sin makes! Adam and Eve's lives changed the moment they ate the fruit. Suddenly they had to hide from each other because they were naked. They hid from God because they knew something wasn't right. They were different, and so was their relationship. We went from a life of a perfect relationship without guilt, shame, and conflict to a life filled with guilt, shame, and conflict.

This need to hide has haunted us since then. We're afraid to let people in to see who we really are. We hide from ourselves because we don't want to know how screwed up we are. We'd rather believe that the problem is outside of us rather than within us.

We live in a broken world with broken people and, as a result, broken relationships. Living in intimate relationships is no longer safe. Insecurity has crept into all of our relationships. We live with the fear of not being good enough, not having what it takes to succeed, and getting hurt by someone. Worry and anxiety permeate our lives. This world no longer feels safe.

Our Relationship with Self Is Broken

I don't know how many times I've said, "You idiot!" when talking about myself. I've also said phrases like, "I can't believe I did it again," or "How stupid can I be?" I'm sure you, the reader, have your own set of words or phases you use for berating yourself.

The issue is that we only use these words and phrases when we screw up. We use them when we don't meet the expectations of others or when we keep doing the same thing wrong over and over again. We feel the weight of failure, and we don't know how to handle it.

I think the implication is that we have done something wrong and we know we have. So we chide ourselves and beat ourselves up until we think we've done it enough and everything is fixed. Justice and judgement have to be served. Sometimes it takes years for this to happen, and sometimes it never happens. We can't let go of it because we've taken the failure on as part of our identity.

The guilt, the shame, and the anger we experience tell us something's wrong. They tell us we're not what we want to be. We know within our being that something is missing.

Sin Broke the Image of God Within Us

Sin broke our relationship with God. It changed the way we relate to the world around us. Intimacy with others has become something that scares us, thanks to sin. We've become scared to look inward because we know we're broken. We're afraid to see the sin that lies within us. In essence, sin has broken the image of God within us.

God created us in His image. He gave us the ability to think, to feel, to make choices, and to live in relationship with Him, others, ourselves, and His creation. Sin broke this image by changing the way we live this image out.

Our Thoughts Toward God Changed

Sin changed the way we think about God. He said everything He created was very good when He finished creation. Adam and Eve knew God as being a good God. They experienced His goodness every day in the Garden. Life was good.

Then they were tempted by the serpent to doubt God's goodness. The serpent told them God was holding out on them and that if they ate the fruit they would be like God. They gave in to the temptation, ate the fruit, and everything instantly changed.

We no longer see God as good. We don't trust God to have our back. We're not sure if He will take care of us. Will He provide for our needs? Often it seems He's not even there. We start to live independently from Him because we don't trust Him to take care of us.

Because God no longer feels safe, we don't seek a deep relationship with Him. God is Holy and can't tolerate or even look at sin. So where does that leave us?

Does God still want us? Will He reject us or welcome us with open arms? Will we be judged and condemned or loved and wanted? It's easier to live self-centered lives that we think we can control than it is to risk being rejected by the One who created us.

Our Feelings Toward God Changed

We've learned to live in fear of God. This fear is expressed in our lives on a continuum. On one end we live in fear that if we do anything wrong, God will strike us dead. So we try to appease an angry and vengeful God. On the other end we live our lives as though God doesn't exist so we don't have to live with the fear anymore.

Most of us live somewhere in the middle of this continuum. Deep within us, we know God exists. Yet we also know that we don't measure up to His standards. We believe we aren't good enough for Him. So we live our lives in uncertainty and insecurity, wondering who God is and if we can still know Him?

Living in this uncertainty and insecurity has bred an anger and bitterness toward God. We get angry when bad things happen to good people. We get angry when natural disasters claim human life and destroy homes. We get angry about the increase in crime, poverty, and homelessness. Some, in turn, become apathetic and unfeeling toward these things.

Yet, we all take this anger and turn it toward God. We ask the question, "Why, God?" as if He owes us an answer. Sometimes God doesn't give us an answer; sometimes we don't like the answer. Either way, we become bitter towards God because He hasn't caused our lives to be the way we want them to be.

Our Choices Toward God Changed

Our choices in following God and living in relationship with Him have changed. Many of us think and feel that God isn't good. He isn't trustworthy to handle our lives and our decisions. Most of the time we don't think God knows what's best for us. We may trust Him in some areas of our lives, but not in those closest to our hearts.

These thoughts and feelings have led us to a point

where we don't seek God. Many don't want anything to do with Him. Paul states it best in Romans 3:10–12 when he writes that there is no one who seeks God. Sin is the reason we seek a life without God. We don't think we need Him.

Since we don't need God, we've made ourselves God just as Adam and Eve did when they ate the fruit. We don't allow God to decide what's right and wrong. We decide it. We deny God His rightful place as Lord and King and put ourselves in His place instead.

We live in a world where everything is relative. There are no moral absolutes. What society says is right today could be wrong tomorrow. We live in a world that is always changing. This change is based on the whims of whomever is in charge.

We have lost a real, solid foundation for our lives by removing God from it. We lose the only foundation that will never change. We have destined ourselves to a life of uncertainty and pain by removing God from His rightful place as Lord and King in our lives and in this world.

Our Relationship with God Was Changed

Sin fundamentally changed our relationship with God. First, our relationship with God changed because it was broken by sin. God is Holy and can't tolerate sin in His presence or even look on it. Sin makes it impossible for us to live in relationship with God, even if we wanted to.

Second, because of sin we don't want to live in relationship with God. We believe God isn't good. We don't think God is trustworthy. Many think He's only out to get us. Why should we follow, or want to follow, someone whom we think or believe doesn't have our best interest at heart?

It seems like God has abandoned us and this world we

live in. As a result, many choose to ignore and not follow God. We feel like we know what is best and God doesn't. We choose to live our lives without God. We're left feeling angry and bitter about life and about God.

If this is what we think of God, feel about God, and choose to do with God, then why would we want a relationship with God? It seems it would be easier to say, "God, go away and leave us alone. We don't need you." For many of us, that's exactly what we do. We live without Him.

Because we have chosen to live life without God, we are left with only one choice for relationship. We are left with only other people and ourselves to have relationships with. This relegates us to a life of pain, heartache, hurt, and uncertainty as we demonstrated earlier.

Our Relationships with Others Changed

In many ways, sin has impacted our relationships with others in the same way it has with God. Our ability to build deep, intimate relationships is broken. We think if people really knew us, they'd judge us and run away. We think we'd be unacceptable because others couldn't handle our true selves.

We live in fear of being exposed as a fraud. We're afraid that others will see we aren't who we say we are. We don't want the ridicule and humiliation we'd feel if we are exposed. We become fearful, anxious, and distrustful of others.

We build walls to keep ourselves safe. We should all join the brick-layer union. We're all great at building walls around ourselves. We build walls to keep others, including God, at a safe distance so we can't get hurt. We live in fear of intimacy. We don't want to leave ourselves open to being rejected or abandoned again.

The problem is that while our walls keep us safe, they also keep us locked in. They prevent us from really getting to know anyone. They keep us in isolation. They keep us from finding the intimacy we really desire.

We wear masks to hide who we really are so we can appear acceptable to others. We do everything we can to present ourselves as acceptable in every situation. We live like it's Halloween everyday, with our hypothetical masks and costumes.

We find ourselves in a paradox. We long for intimacy and to be known, but this brings the risk of being exposed and our having our masks ripped off. Instead, we choose to live life with walls we create to keep us safe from getting hurt. We were created for relationship and intimacy, but instead we live lives of isolation and loneliness.

It's no wonder that addiction sounds so appealing. It says, "Come here and indulge me. I will ease your fear of exposure. I will give you a place where you can feel safe and forget your loneliness. I will be the only friend you need."

The problem is addiction doesn't offer a real solution to our deepest worries, fears, and anxieties. In the end it only adds to them. Addiction gives us a temporary and false sense of control and power that it immediately withdraws when we stop indulging in it.

Our Relationship with Self Changed

Before sin came into the world, Adam and Eve knew who they were. I don't believe they used words like *idiot* or *stupid* or used phrases like "I can't believe I did it again" before they ate the fruit. I don't think they knew what it was like to feel the guilt and shame we feel today. They lived in a garden that was good. All was right in their world.

Adam and Eve decided this wasn't enough though. They bought the lie that they could be like God, so ate the fruit, and sin came and broke everything. Sin broke their relationship with God and others. It also broke their relationship with themselves.

When God confronted Adam and Eve in Genesis 3:8–13, Adam and Eve's response is classic. Adam said they knew they were naked, so they hid. They knew they were different after eating the fruit. I believe they felt guilt and shame for the first time. I also believe they hid so they wouldn't be exposed as being different. They knew who they were before they ate the fruit. They were acceptable to God and lived in relationship with Him. After they ate the fruit, they didn't have a clue if they would still be accepted by God.

I think we all can relate to this feeling of not being what we know we are supposed to be. As was pointed out earlier, there is a hole inside each of us, and it's telling us we aren't perfect. I believe this is the source of the guilt and shame we all feel.

Instead of looking for what we have done right, we almost always focus on what we've done wrong. It only takes one negative criticism to cancel out fifty compliments. Ever wonder why this is true? I believe it is easier to accept negative criticism as true because negative criticism fits the way we see ourselves. We can accept negative criticism because we aren't perfect. It fits what we know about ourselves. We can't accept compliments well because they don't fit.

We live in a paradox called life. Life forces us to make

choices that impact others and ourselves. These choices may be between what's right or wrong. We must decide if we want to hurt or not hurt others. We must decide if we want to experience pain or not.

Many times, we know what we should do, but we don't do it. Why don't we do what we should do? The answer to this question haunts us on a daily basis. It is the source of the guilt and shame we live with.

This difference between who we are and want to be and what we act like is enormous. But one thing I believe is true is that we don't want to know why the gap exists.

We do what Adam and Eve did. We blame everyone else. We can't admit we are the problem. It's easier for us to judge in others what we see in ourselves: "It's not my fault that something happened." "If the other person hadn't done what they did, this never would have happened." Or, "If I only had this, then things would be different." Instead of living with a sense of confidence, worth, relationship, and purpose, we live in a state of fear, anger, and anxiety. We know there is something wrong with us, but we just can't admit it. We live in a paradox of knowing what we want to be, but we can't live it out. It is an empty place to live we were never intended to experience.

Indulging our addictions allows us to avoid this disappointment, this emptiness that characterizes our lives. It allows us to numb the pain and for a moment to feel whole, but it never lasts.

My Story

I've felt the full weight of sin in my life. I've had problems with intimacy my whole life. I've lived through numerous codependent relationships. I used pornography to avoid having to relate to women. In the end, I never found anything but never-ending loneliness.

I came to hate who I was. I looked at what God created in me and called it trash. My guilt and shame at not being what I wanted to be added to my self-condemnation. I knew I was smart, but that wasn't cool. I dumbed myself down and hated that too.

I never felt good enough for anyone. I was always the butt of my friends' jokes. I was physically and emotionally abused at home and in school. I was sexually abused by a neighbor. I always felt like the odd man out at church and in the Christian organizations I was involved with. I can't count the number times I thought about committing suicide.

I share all of this to show you that I am no different than you. We may not have the exact same stories, but we have all suffered because of sin. No one is exempt.

The key thing I want you to take away is that if it weren't for God not giving up on me, I would have. I can state as fact that God hasn't given up on you either. We can think we have no hope, feel like we have no hope, and make a choice to live like we have no hope for a better life. We have proven this true if our hope was only in ourselves to find it.

God, however, offers us something different. God offers us hope for a better life. A hope for a life of meaning and significance. God offers us a life of restored relationship with Him, others, and ourselves. We'll take a look at this hope in the next chapter.

Scripture References

Romans 8:20–21
"For the creation was subjected to futility, not willingly, but because of Him who subjected it, in hope that the creation itself also will be set free from its slavery to corruption into the freedom of the glory of the children of God."

Psalm 5:4–5
"For You are not a God who takes pleasure in wickedness;
No evil dwells with You.
The boastful shall not stand before Your eyes;
You hate all who do iniquity."

Psalm 26:4–5
"I do not sit with deceitful men,
Nor will I go with pretenders.
I hate the assembly of evildoers,
And I will not sit with the wicked."

Habakkuk 1:13
"Your eyes are too pure to approve evil,
And You can not look on wickedness with favor.
Why do You look with favor

On those who deal treacherously?
Why are You silent when the wicked swallow up
Those more righteous than they?"

Isaiah 64:6
"For all of us have become like one who is unclean,
And all our righteous deeds are like a filthy
   garment;
And all of us wither like a leaf,
And our iniquities, like the wind, take us away."

Genesis 2:25
"And the man and his wife were both naked and
   were not ashamed."

Romans 3:10–12
"There is none righteous, not even one;
There is none who understands, there is none who
   seeks for God;
All have turned aside, together they have become
   useless; There is none who does good, there is
   not even one."

Genesis 3:8–13
"They heard the sound of the LORD God walking

in the garden in the cool of the day, and the man and his wife hid themselves from the presence of the Lord God among the trees of the garden. Then the Lord God called to the man, and said to him, 'Where are you?' He said, 'I heard the sound of You in the garden, and I was afraid because I was naked; so I hid myself.' And He said, 'Who told you that you were naked? Have you eaten from the tree of which I commanded you not to eat?' The man said, 'The woman whom You gave *to be* with me, she gave me from the tree, and I ate.' Then the Lord God said to the woman, 'What is this you have done?' And the woman said, 'The serpent deceived me, and I ate.'"

5

IS THIS ALL WE CAN HOPE FOR?

Hope is passion for what is possible.
—Søren Kierkegaard

God is the source of life. Life without God is hopeless. But life with God is an endless hope.
—*Lailah Gifty Akita*

Hope is one thing that is essential to life. We use hope in so many ways. We say, "I hope things work out." "I hope I can get that promotion." "I hope I can find my soul mate." For many of us who suffered something tragic, we say, "I hope I can survive today."

I think hope is critical to living. Proverbs 13:12 warns us that when we lose hope, life becomes difficult to live. Depression, anxiety, and even suicide can result from losing hope. Proverbs also instructs that maintaining hope in our lives can result in a life worth living. I believe that's why Paul includes it with love and faith in 1 Corinthians 13:13. A hope based in love produces a faith that allows us to endure the chaos that life throws at us.

Hope is elusive for many of us. We hope for lives that are safe, secure, and meaningful. Yet, sadly, we end up with lives characterized by feeling unsafe, insecure, and insignificant. We live broken lives, in broken relationships, and in a broken world. Our lives are a dim reflection of what we hope for and were created for.

Hope for me was always a dangerous thing. I hoped for a life where I didn't feel alone and worthless. I didn't feel like I was worthy or deserved that kind of life. So I pretended these things could be true. I turned to sports, but that didn't give me what I was looking for. I turned to "living as a good Christian," which failed miserably. I eventually got married and had a family, but that didn't work either.

In my hopelessness I contemplated suicide. I believed I was destined to live a life of misery. I was feeling what many, if not all of us, feel at some point during our lives. I lost hope because I thought this was the end of my story.

God, however, says it's not the end of our stories. He wants to write a new chapter in our lives if we will let Him. He states there is hope for us to find the life He created us to live, but we have to want it. This hope is found in the Gospel, which is God's plan for the redemption and restoration of His relationship with us.

Sin doesn't have to have the last word in our lives.

What to Do with Sin?

The way I see it, God had three choices to deal with sin. He could have eliminated creation and started over. He could have abandoned us to ourselves. Or He could pay the cost to be in relationship with us.

First, God could've said to Adam and Eve, "Okay you both screwed up and sinned. So I'm going to start over. See ya!" He could have obliterated His creation and started over. This choice would remove sin from His presence. His righteousness, justice, and holiness would be satisfied, but it wouldn't restore His reputation of being good and loving. It wouldn't satisfy His desire for relationship with us. It would have eliminated us and any possibility for relationship with us.

God's second choice was to leave us on our own and walk away. God could've said, "You both want to be Me? Have at it. I'm out of here! See ya!" This, too, would've eliminated sin. God wouldn't have sin in His presence, but neither would He have us in His presence. Again, no us, no relationship.

Since God wants relationship with us, God was left with only one choice. He had to pay the price for our sin, and that price is death. We are told in Genesis 2:17 that the consequence of eating the fruit is death. Romans 6:23 tells us that the wages of sin is death. God had to be willing to die to pay for our sins to restore relationship with us.

The Gospel Is God's Answer to Sin

The Gospel is God's powerful response to sin. It is a story of hope for our redemption and restoration. The Gospel paints a picture of God's great love for us and the extent He is willing to go to restore relationship with us. This picture is of God's love for us because He was willing to send Jesus Christ to die to pay the cost, or ransom, for our sins.

Romans 5:6-10 teaches us that God demonstrated His love for us by sending His Son Jesus Christ to die for our sins, even though we were His enemies because of our sins. How many of us would be willing to send our only child to die for our worst enemy to save our enemy's life? Yet, God did just that for us. 1 John 4:9-10 reveals His love for us by sending Jesus Christ into the world because He loved us before we could love Him. It wasn't because of anything we did, but simply because God loved us first.

The Gospel shows the extent God was willing to go to redeem and restore His relationship with us. Death is not only the penalty for sin, but it is also required to redeem and restore us to a relationship with God. Hebrews 9:22 teaches us that without the shedding of blood, there is no forgiveness of sin. A sacrifice was required for our sins to be forgiven.

Leviticus 1:1–5 describes what a sacrifice for sin looks like. First, the sacrifice must be a male animal without spot or blemish. It had to be perfect. Second, the person making the sacrifice had to place a hand on the head of the sacrifice so that the blood shed by the sacrifice would cover the person's sin. Finally, the animal is killed so blood is shed for the forgiveness of sins.

This is why it's clear from God's point of view that we can't pay for our own sins. We are not perfect. Our sins go before us. We can't do enough good things because there is no shedding of blood in those things. We can't meet the requirements needed to be an acceptable sacrifice in God's eyes. We would be without hope if God didn't do it for us.

Jesus Christ: God's Plan and Our Only Hope

The good news is that God made away for our sins to be forgiven. God the Father sent God the Son, Jesus Christ, to be the sacrifice for our sins. Jesus' death on the cross paid the ultimate price for sin.

Jesus Christ was able to be the ultimate sacrifice because He was perfect. Jesus lived a perfect life without sin. Jesus could die for sin because He was sinless. Like the animal sacrifice in Leviticus, Jesus was able to take on our sins because He had none of His own. 2 Corinthians 5:21 teaches that God took Jesus, who was without sin, and made Him a sin offering for us.

Because Jesus was the ultimate sacrifice, the blood He shed on the cross is the source of our forgiveness. Matthew 26:28 reveals that Jesus' blood was shed for the forgiveness of many. Ephesians 1:7 reminds us that our redemption and forgiveness come from the blood Jesus shed on the cross. Colossians 1:19–20 says we were reconciled to God through Jesus' shed blood.

Jesus' death on the cross also opened the door for us to experience God's mercy. Mercy simply means that we don't get what we deserve. God's mercy can be ours because of Jesus' death on the cross. Ephesians 2:4–5 teaches us that God has said we no longer have to pay the penalty for sin because He has already done it. His mercy is greater than our sin. God has made it possible for us to not get what we deserve, which is death. His mercy has made it possible for us to be declared not guilty in His presence.

Most of us have no idea of what mercy is because the church doesn't often talk about mercy. Yet, the importance of mercy is unmistakable. Titus 3:5 points out that we are not saved by what we do, but according to God's mercy. 1 Peter 1:3 teaches that without God's great mercy we have no hope.

Understanding God's mercy is critical to understanding the Gospel.

Jesus' death on the cross is only one part of the Gospel. His resurrection from the dead is the other. It's the resurrection that separates Christianity from all other religions. It's because of the Resurrection that two things happen allowing God to restore and redeem us.

First, 1 Peter 1:3 makes it clear it is through the Resurrection that we are saved and restored to relationship with God. Jesus' resurrection opened the door for us to experience God's saving grace.

Ephesians 2:5 reminds us that we are saved by grace. It's because of God's mercy and love for us that He has made His grace available to us through Jesus' resurrection. It is by grace we are saved! Ephesians 2:8–9 teaches us we can't do anything to earn it. Grace is God's gift to us. God's grace isn't based on what we do—but grace can be ours because God loves us.

So what is grace? Grace has been defined in many ways through the years. The best definition I've come across is simple. Grace means we get what we don't deserve. We deserve to be separated from God because of our sins. We don't deserve to live in relationship with God. Yet, because of His love for us, God's grace can save us from being separated from God. God's Grace makes it possible for God to restore us to relationship with Him.

Second, Jesus' resurrection makes it possible for us to live a new life. John 10:10 says that one of the reasons Jesus came was so we could have life and have it abundantly. Jesus came to do what this world can't do. He came to restore us to a life that has meaning and purpose. Romans 6:4 reminds us that Jesus was resurrected so that in Him we can live a new life.

Jesus came to show us what it means to be loved and how to love. He came to show how important we are to God, what we are worth to God, and to restore the dignity that is ours because we are created in God's image. Jesus made all this possible by restoring God's relationship with us through God's grace, which is made available to us through His resurrection.

I became inoculated to the Gospel growing up in church. I heard about God's love for me so much I began to take it for granted. Jesus being born at Christmas began to mean what presents I was going to get more than His birth. I looked forward to Christmas break more than celebrating Jesus. Easter meant a week off from school and Good Friday became just another day to go to church. I began to think I was saved just because I went to church and completed confirmation.

It wasn't until I was a sophomore in high school that I made a decision to put my faith in the Gospel. Even then, I still didn't really understand what I had done. I knew I was saved, but now what? I didn't understand the promises contained in the Gospel because no one took the time to explain them to me.

So I put my hope in getting married, having a family, a good job, a home, and being good enough for others and God. That was what it meant to me to be a successful man. Yet, I discovered all of these things eventually let me down. My hopes were crushed because these things don't have the power to do what I wanted them to do. They couldn't make me whole or fix my life.

It wasn't until about seven years ago—when I started

explain the Gospel to others suffering from addictions—that I really began to understand the its true meaning. I began to understand the freedom from guilt and shame that is available to anyone who wants it. I started to understand how to live the abundant life Jesus promised to all who want it.

The Gospel has given me a new perspective on life and a solid foundation to come back to when things go wrong or when I screw things up. Understanding the Gospel has helped me to start to know what it means to be whole and change my life. Since I know all of my sins are forgiven because of God's mercy and grace, I can now live a new life. I can face life from a position of strength in Jesus instead of weakness and fear without Him.

This new life in Jesus also brings me hope because it is based in the character of God and not me. Numbers 23:19, Hebrews 13:8, and Revelations 1:8 and 22:13 all teach that God doesn't change. He remains the same yesterday, today, and tomorrow. Since the Gospel is based in what God has done, then the Gospel will always provide an unchanging and solid foundation for our lives.

I find hope in the fact the Gospel is steadfast. It means that I can have a relationship with God through Jesus Christ that will never change because the foundation of this relationship will never change or crumble. I know that I won't remain the same as my foundation for my life is changed and rebuilt by God through the Gospel.

How Can I Get What the Gospel Offers for My Life?

It is true that God made it possible for us to have our sins forgiven and to be restored to relationship with Him. God made His solution available to all of us. God did His part. However, God doesn't force us to accept His solution. He gives us the option to either accept or reject His solution.

Romans 10:8–13 teaches us several things about the Gospel. First, the Gospel can save us. Romans 1:16–17 supports this by stating that the Gospel is the power of God for salvation for all who believe it. Second, we have to confess that Jesus is Lord. We must believe that Jesus is the only one who can save us and that we can't save ourselves. We can't be good enough on our own to save ourselves from our sins. Third, we have to believe in our hearts that God raised Jesus from the dead. We need to acknowledge it was through Jesus' death and resurrection we can find the forgiveness of our sins and the restoration of our relationship with God.

If you are willing to admit you can't save yourself from your sin, recognize that you can't earn God's grace and mercy, and that only through Jesus' death and resurrection can we find the salvation we long for, then all you need to do is ask for it. Romans 10:13 teaches us all we need to do is call upon, or ask, Jesus to save us.

It is as simple as praying: **Lord Jesus, save me, a sinner**.

A great example of this is the thief who was crucified next to Jesus. One began yelling insults at Jesus. The second interrupted the first and said they were justly dying for what they did, but to Jesus he asked that Jesus to remember him, i.e. save him, when Jesus came into His kingdom.

Jesus replied that today the thief would be with Him in paradise. Jesus told the thief that his sins would be forgiven and he would be with Jesus in paradise simply because he asked. The thief didn't have to do anything, change his life, or live as a good person. He couldn't, he was dying. All he had to do was ask (Luke 23:39–43).

It is the same for you. The best example I know of goes like this. I offer you a pen and say, "Here I want you to have it." You gladly take it. First, you needed to believe that I had the pen. Second, you needed to believe that I wanted you to have the pen. Finally, you took the pen believing that I would give it to you. You exercised faith in taking the pen. Acts 2:21 teaches that all who call on the name of the Jesus will be saved.

This is how the Gospel meets us where we are. The Gospel promises that our lives can be made whole. It promises a new life that satisfies our deepest longings. It provides hope for now and the future. It promises acceptance, redemption, and restoration to all who put their faith in it.

When we ask Jesus to forgive us we change. Our lives are not the same because we are no longer known by what we've done with our lives, but by what Jesus has done for us. We become "new creations" in Jesus (1 Corinthians 5:17). So what are these new things that are true of us? We'll take a look at these in the next two chapters.

Scripture References

Proverbs 13:12
"Hope deferred makes the heart sick, But desire fulfilled is a tree of life."

1 Corinthians 13:13
"But now faith, hope, love, abide these three; but the greatest of these is love."

Genesis 2:17
"but from the tree of the knowledge of good and evil you shall not eat, for in the day that you eat from it you will surely die."

Romans 6:23
"For the wages of sin is death, but the free gift of God is eternal life in Christ Jesus our Lord."

Romans 5:6–10
"For while we were still helpless, at the right time Christ died for the ungodly. For one will hardly die for a righteous man; though perhaps for the good man someone would dare even to die. But God demonstrates His own love toward us, in that while we were yet sinners, Christ died for us. Much more then, having now been justified by His blood, we shall be saved from the wrath of God through Him. For if while we were enemies we were reconciled to God through the death of His Son, much more, having been reconciled, we shall be saved by His life."

1 John 4:9–10
"By this the love of God was manifested in us, that God has sent His only begotten Son into the world so that we might live through Him. In this is love, not that we loved God, but that He loved us and sent His Son to be the propitiation for our sins."

Hebrews 9:22
"And according to the Law, one may almost say, all things are cleansed with blood, and without shedding of blood there is no forgiveness."

Leviticus 1:3–5
"If his offering is a burnt offering from the herd, he shall offer it, a male without defect; he shall offer it at the doorway of the tent of meeting, that he may be accepted before the Lord. 'He shall lay his hand on the head of the burnt offering, that it may be accepted for him to make atonement on his behalf. 'He shall slay the young bull before the Lord; and Aaron's sons the priests shall offer up the blood and sprinkle the blood around on the altar that is at the doorway of the tent of meeting."

2 Corinthians 5:17
"Therefore if anyone is in Christ, he is a new creature; the old things passed away; behold, new things have come."

Matthew 26:28
"for this is My blood of the covenant, which is poured out for many for forgiveness of sins."

Ephesians 1:7
"In Him we have redemption through His blood, the forgiveness of our trespasses, according to the riches of His grace."

Colossians 1:19–20
"For it was the Father's good pleasure for all the fullness to dwell in Him, and through Him to reconcile all things to Himself, having made peace through the blood of His cross; through Him, I say, whether things on earth or things in heaven."

Ephesians 2:4–5
"But God, being rich in mercy, because of His great

love with which He loved us, even when we were dead in our transgressions, made us alive together with Christ (by grace you have been saved)."

Titus 3:5
"He saved us, not on the basis of deeds which we have done in righteousness, but according to His mercy, by the washing of regeneration and renewing by the Holy Spirit."

1 Peter 1:3
"Blessed be the God and Father of our Lord Jesus Christ, who according to His great mercy has caused us to be born again to a living hope through the resurrection of Jesus Christ from the dead."

Ephesians 2:4-5
"But God, being rich in mercy, because of His great love with which He loved us, even when we were dead in our transgressions, made us alive together with Christ (by grace you have been saved)."

Ephesians 2:8–9
"For by grace you have been saved through faith;
and that not of yourselves, it is the gift of God;
not as a result of works, so that no one may
boast."

John 10:10
"The thief comes only to steal and kill and destroy;
I came that they may have life, and have it
abundantly."

Numbers 23:19
"God is not a man, that He should lie,
Nor a son of man, that He should repent;
Has He said, and will He not do it?
Or has He spoken, and will He not make it good?"

Hebrews 13:8
"Jesus Christ is the same yesterday and today and
forever."

Revelation 22:13
"I am the Alpha and the Omega, the first and the
last, the beginning and the end."

Romans 10:8–13

"But what does it say? 'The word is near you, in your mouth and in your heart'—that is, the word of faith which we are preaching, that if you confess with your mouth Jesus as Lord, and believe in your heart that God raised Him from the dead, you will be saved; for with the heart a person believes, resulting in righteousness, and with the mouth he confesses, resulting in salvation. For the Scripture says, 'Whoever believes in Him will not be disappointed.' For there is no distinction between Jew and Greek; for the same Lord is Lord of all, abounding in riches for all who call on Him; for 'Whoever will call on the name of the Lord will be saved.'"

Romans 1:16

"For I am not ashamed of the gospel, for it is the power of God for salvation to everyone who believes, to the Jew first and also to the Greek."

Luke 23:39–43

"One of the criminals who were hanged there was hurling abuse at Him, saying, 'Are You not the Christ? Save Yourself and us!' But the other answered, and rebuking him said, 'Do you not even fear God, since you are under the same sentence of condemnation? "And we indeed are suffering justly, for we are receiving what we deserve for our deeds; but this man has done nothing wrong." And he was saying, 'Jesus, remember me when You come in Your kingdom!' And He said to him, 'Truly I say to you, today you shall be with Me in Paradise.'"

Acts 2:21
"And it shall be that everyone who calls on the name of the Lord will be saved."

2 Corinthians 5:17
"Therefore if anyone is in Christ, he is a new creature; the old things passed away; behold, new things have come."

6

WHAT HAPPENS NOW?

The Christian does not think God will love us because we are good, but that God will make us good because He loves us.
—C.S. Lewis

Being a Christian is more than just an instantaneous conversion; it is like a daily process whereby you grow to be more and more like Christ.
—Billy Graham

Everything changes when we put our faith in the Gospel and what Jesus did for us. We are made new. We become children of God. We are saved from our sins. There are many things that change about us when Jesus forgives our sins and gives us new life. In the next two chapters I will focus on what I consider the six most significant truths that happen to all who become Christians.

God Becomes Lord and King in Our Lives

I think many Christians have a problem with the first, and most important, change that takes place when we're saved by Jesus. When we ask Jesus to save us, we are giving Him permission and the right to change our lives. We pledge our allegiance to Him as Lord and King in our lives.

All of us, not just those who suffer from addiction, want to be in control of our lives. We need to feel like we have power over what happens to us and what we do in life. We hate feeling powerless and out of control.

Being out of control and powerless means we are at the mercy of someone else. It means someone else can do whatever they want to do to us or ask whatever they want of us, and we have to do it or face the consequences.

This is what I thought pledging my allegiance God as Lord and King in my life meant. I believed God was sitting in heaven and looking down on me to beat me into submission. I thought God had a list of dos and don'ts I had to follow or else He would punish me every time I screwed up.

I thought I had to look good, be a "good person," and meet God's expectations or pay the price. It is really easy to buy into seeing God this way. God may have saved me by grace and mercy, but that doesn't mean He has to accept me or even like me. This view of God has been foundational to my life for years.

I developed this view from misunderstanding Philippians 2:12–13. Many focus on verse 12, which teaches that we work out our salvation. If we focus only on this aspect, it sounds like we have to perform. It places the responsibility for change in our lives squarely on us. It also teaches that we should do this in fear and trembling, which to me paints a picture of us cowering in the presence of an Almighty God, ready to punish us at any moment.

We miss the point, however, if we place our emphasis on verse 12 and not verse 13. We do need to work out our salvation through obedience and discipleship, but not in fear of being punished. Instead, we work out our salvation in awe and reverence of an Almighty God who loves us enough to die for us and who is at work in us to enable us to do what He wants and to please Him.

Verse 13 teaches that it's God who is at work in us, enabling us to do His will. It is God's desire for us to live out His will, so He is working to make this possible for all who are saved by Jesus. God knows the only way we can find the life we all desire—one of hope and significance—is if we're following His will for our lives.

Being in Awe and Reverence

Our responsibility is to grow in our salvation by living in awe and reverence of who God is as He works in us. My wife and I were on a bird watching trip to Gambell on St. Lawrence Island in Alaska. I was sitting at the Bering Sea sea watch and felt amazed as I watched the waves roll in. I witnessed such power and beauty no man could ever control or tame. At the same time, I also felt a deep sense of peace and comfort in knowing something bigger than me was in control of what I saw.

This is what I think it means to be in awe of God. To be in awe of God is to recognize He is the Creator of this world. His power and beauty are displayed for all to see.

God is all-powerful. His power remains unmatched by anyone or anything. That day by the ocean, I was reminded how small I am in light of God's power and beauty. I stood in awe as I watched the waves crash onto the shore.

I'm in awe of God's love, His grace, and His mercy. God could've destroyed us because of our sin, but because of His great love for us He chose not to. Instead, He chose to make it possible for our sins to be forgiven and for us to be restored to relationship with Him.

I believe the only response to being in awe of God is reverence. Reverence means to have a deep respect and honor for someone. It's acknowledging the person we're in awe of is greater than us and deserves our respect and honor. God has proven He is worthy of our reverence through what He accomplished for us through the death and resurrection of Jesus.

Verse 13 has a second, and just as important, focus. God enables us to not only do His will, but to do His good pleasure as well. Ephesians 2:10 teaches that God has good works for us to accomplish in Jesus that He prepared in advance so we can do them. It's God's good pleasure to enable us to do these works.

God gives us the ability to live a life that pleases Him. 1 Corinthians 12:4–6 teaches God has given each of us our own unique set of skills, strengths, and gifts. He teaches us how to use them so we can accomplish the good works He has for us to do. God's good pleasure is to watch His children live out His will for their lives as He has enabled them.

Following God's will for our lives doesn't mean everything will be sunshine and roses. We live in a broken world. We are guaranteed that we will suffer and be hurt from being abused, used, and abandoned. God promises we won't suffer alone or for nothing. Jesus is with us always (Matthew 28:20). He does promise to bring good out of our suffering (Genesis 50:20; Romans 8:28).

It is God's good pleasure for us to live out His will for our lives, but how do we know what His will is for our lives? What is it He wants to accomplish through us and in us? Inquiring minds have been asking these questions for centuries.

God's Will for Every Believer

I think His will for us can be found in three verses. The first two are found in Romans 8:28–29, which teach that it is God's will that we be changed to reflect who Jesus is to the world around us. God wants to restore and redeem the unique skills, gifts, and strengths He has given us so we can reflect who Jesus is in our own unique way.

The third verse is found in Philippians 1:6. It teaches that we can be confident God will change us to reflect who Jesus is. God will bring these changes to completion when Jesus comes back. Until then we're a work in progress, both as the church and as individuals.

This gives me a feeling of security and hope. It gives me a sense of security because I know God's not giving up on me. He will continue to work in me to change me to reflect who Jesus is as long as I'm alive on this planet. It gives me hope because I can be confident and know for certain that one day I will be all that God created me to be, which is even more than I can imagine..

Yet, knowing all this, I've struggled with pledging my allegiance to God as Lord and King of my life. I've struggled with it because it was hard for me to submit to a God who allowed all the crap I've experienced and done in my life. Yes, God could've stopped all of it and eliminated the suffering I've experienced and caused, but He chose not to.

Yet, it's this very fact that God did allow it to happen has started to change the way I see Him. I wouldn't be who I am today if He had prevented my trials and suffering. I wouldn't be writing this book if He hadn't allowed the adversity I've experienced. I wouldn't be able to be effective as a counselor because I wouldn't be able to empathize with others in their suffering.

God is bringing good out of the suffering I've experienced and caused. He has proven He is greater than all my suffering. He has proven to me He is able to carry me through life in ways my addictions never could. The courage and strength I have found in Him has proven better for facing life's chaos than my addictions. I am learning to trust God's heart as He changes my heart. The Gospel is the greatest proof that His heart toward me is one of love and longing for relationship with me.

I am learning to pledge my allegiance to Him more every day. I'm learning to trust in God's goodness because I'm seeing it in my own life and in the lives of others. I'm continuing to learn in the midst of life's chaos that I can trust in God's goodness and His love for me. I'm committed to pledging my allegiance to Him as the Lord and King of my life.

We Are Forgiven

A second thing happens to us when we ask Jesus to save us. All of our sins are forgiven. Hebrews 8:12, 10:17, and Jeremiah 31:31–34 teach that God chooses to not remember our sins anymore.

I find it hard to fully comprehend that an infinite, Holy,

Righteous, and all-knowing God would choose to not remember my sins. If God is all-knowing, then how can He not know I've sinned? How does He ignore something that I'm well aware of? The short answer is, He doesn't ignore them. He chooses not to remember them.

Some say that God chooses to forgive and to "forget" our sins. I have a problem with this. Our sins are out there for all to see. I believe that for God to forget them means He just ignores them as if they didn't exist. He isn't intentional in dealing with our sin, He just forgets.

I don't believe this is supported in Scripture. Scripture teaches that He chooses not to remember our sins. He makes an intentional, volitional choice not to remember our sins. God is a compassionate and loving God; He has separated our sins from us as far as the east is from the west (Psalm 103:8–12; Isaiah 43:25; 1 John 1:9).

I believe *how* God does this is found in *who* God is. We must remember: God has created all things, including time and space. God is outside of time and space because He created them. He isn't limited by them as we are. The beginning and the end of time and space are the same to God (Revelation 22:13).

Since God is already present at the end of time and space, so are we. God sees us as we will be at that time. God sees us as the perfect, righteous, sinless people we were supposed to be from the beginning. God sees the shed blood of Christ that covers us and removes our sins and chooses not to remember them.

This is important for us to learn and remember. Even though God sees us as we will be in the day of Christ's return, He also knows we are stuck in time and space. God knows we will still sin. This is why understanding we are forgiven of <u>all our sins, including future ones,</u> is so important. God's mercy cancels our guilt, and His grace takes away our shame.

This gives new meaning to Philippians 1:6 for me. It gives me hope that my future doesn't have to look like my past. God starts a new, good work in each person who asks Jesus to forgive their sins. This work of God is transforming us from the inside out.

The focus of this good work is to change us to reflect who Jesus is. God wants to change the way we think and feel about who He is, how we view His plans for our lives, and His intentions toward us. In short, He wants us to see Him as the good God He is.

God wants us to see ourselves as He does, both as a work in progress in this life and what He already sees us as in the future. God wants us to experience the abundant life Jesus promised in John 10:10 and to start to live life fearlessly because He is with us.

However, being forgiven for our sins by God doesn't take away the consequences of our sins. We still pay the price for sins. We still suffer the consequences of our sins—broken relationships, poor health, and incarceration, to name a few. What forgiveness does promise is that we don't have to face our consequences alone.

I must admit I don't always remember this. It's easy to forget when I think about all the times I've hurt others and sinned against God. I feel like David did when he wrote in Psalm 51:3–4 that he was always aware of his sin and that God was right when He judged him for it.

Yet, it's in the midst of remembering my sin that I'm finding the Gospel to be enough to help me. When I am reminded of something I've done, I choose to remind myself that it is already forgiven in Jesus. By learning to accept God's forgiveness in Jesus, I'm learning to live free from the condemnation, guilt, and shame I've suffered from my entire life. I'm able to forgive myself by accepting God's forgiveness for me.

We Are No Longer Outcasts

I think one of the hardest things about living with our addictions is feeling alone and isolated. We feel like no one wants us around because we've wounded everyone so deeply they've disowned us. Many feel condemned by family and those they called friends. We start to feel like outcasts who have no safe place to call home.

The Gospel promises us something different. It promises we can have a safe place to call home. It promises we don't have to live our lives in isolation or alone. Those who are in Jesus are now part of the family of God (Romans 8:15–16). We belong to God's family, but what does this mean?

We Don't Have to Feel Condemned Anymore

God's desire was not to condemn us but to save us (John 3:16–17). God's choice to show us His mercy and grace through Jesus' death and Jesus' resurrection demonstrates His desire to restore His relationship with us, not condemn us. God wants us to live in relationship with Him and not to be condemned to a life without Him.

Romans 7:13–25 shows us where our guilt and shame originate and explains why God's mercy and grace are so important. It teaches that we know the right thing to do, but we often don't do it. James 4:17 also supports this when it teaches that we sin when we don't do the good we know we should do. We feel guilty about not doing what we know is right and suffer from the shame of not doing it.

This guilt and shame leads us to condemn ourselves by beating ourselves up for not doing what we know we should. We know we shouldn't give into our addictions. We know we shouldn't be hurting our families, friends, and ourselves. We start to feel the condemnation of others through their judging us for how we let them down and hurt them. We become our own worst critics and ruthlessly beat ourselves up for what we've done.

I think the key verse in the Romans passage is found in verse 24. Paul asks the question of who can save us from the guilt, shame, and condemnation we live with on a daily basis? He asks who can set us free from this life of contradiction and set us free to live the life we so desire? He answers the question in verse 25: Jesus Christ is able to do this.

There is no condemnation for those who ask Jesus to save them (Romans 8:1). God no longer condemns us because His mercy and grace have covered our sins and restored us to relationship with Him. God chooses to forgive our sins and not condemn us because of what Jesus' death on the cross has accomplished.

God is the one who justifies us, so there is no room for anyone, including ourselves, to accuse us (Romans 8:33–34). It is Jesus who intercedes for us; therefore there is no room for anyone, including ourselves, to condemn us.

So why do we continue living as if we are still condemned when we aren't? This is a question I struggle with every day. Many times I choose to feel condemned by God, others and myself, even though I don't have to. I choose to beat myself up over the smallest things. I choose to live with the guilt and shame.

Yet, as I'm learning to apply the Gospel to my life, I'm finding that I beat myself up less. I remind myself that God doesn't condemn me and I don't have to either. I'm finding it easier to live in relationship with God and myself.

I'm finding the life I've always wanted because I don't have to worry about being perfect. I'm learning I can accept who I am and the things I've done without having to condemn myself for them. I'm learning to live life free from all the guilt and shame I've endured my entire life.

We Are Accepted

Acceptance is something we all long for. It can be the hardest thing to find and the easiest thing to lose. One day we're accepted by others; the next day we aren't because of something we did or didn't do. It's hard to gain back acceptance once we lose it.

Some struggle to gain acceptance because of racism, discrimination, and prejudice. Disabilities, deformities, and mental health disorders put up walls to people being accepted.

Our addictions can make us unacceptable. Ending up in jail or prison, getting drunk or high to the point of not remembering anything, and putting our addictions above everyone else are just a few of the ways others lose respect for us.

Being accepted by God is different. God accepts us the moment we ask Jesus to save us. He doesn't look at what we do or who we are when He considers accepting us.

We need to accept each other just as Jesus accepted us (Romans 15:7). So, what does it mean Jesus has accepted us? When did He accept us?

First, it is important to recognize and accept that Jesus

has accepted us. Our sins aren't enough to stop Him from doing this. Our sins are forgiven as soon as we ask Jesus to save us. The only stumbling block to our being accepted is removed, and we now have a relationship with God through Jesus.

Second, God's acceptance of us isn't based on anything we do. It's not based on how we've lived our lives. It's not based on religion, race, sex, orientation, or any other individual characteristic. It's based on Jesus' death and resurrection (Colossians 3:11). It's based on the blood Jesus shed on the cross, which covers our sins.

Third, His acceptance of us is complete and full. We are accepted when we ask Jesus to save us. We are accepted as we are, before we could do anything different, say anything different, or think anything different. We are accepted with all our baggage and issues.

What amazes me is that God is glorified because Jesus has accepted us. The angels in heaven rejoice when someone asks Jesus to save them (Luke 15:10). They don't look down and say, "Well, what took you so long." No, they rejoice with God and give Him the praise and adoration He deserves.

Those of us in His church here on earth and in heaven rejoice and praise God when someone is saved. We acknowledge and honor God's goodness because He has saved someone. We praise His name because of His faithfulness to save those who come to Him and ask.

We Are Wanted by God

All of us who suffer from addictions know what it is to not be wanted. Many of us have been disowned by family members, ostracized by our friends, and berated by police and medical personnel. Many of us don't like to be alone with ourselves because the thoughts and memories that come to us are painful to deal with. Feeling unwanted becomes a common and everyday experience.

God, however, says something different. He says He wants us. It's an amazing thing to consider that God, who is perfect, holy, and the Creator of all things, would want to have us around. One example in the Old Testament teaches that God desires a relationship with His children in Jeremiah 24:7. It teaches that God wants to be their God and for them to be His people.

John 14:1–3 paints a more intimate picture. In this passage, Jesus is telling His disciples that He is leaving to prepare a place for them to live in His Father's house. He goes on to tell them that He will be coming back to get them and take them to live with Him there.

Jesus uses the imagery of a Jewish wedding to paint the picture. In a Jewish wedding, the bride and groom come together and host a big engagement party. The groom goes home with his family afterward and the bride remains with her family. While home, the groom must build a house near his father's house. He can't go back to get his bride until it is ready for her. The groom, however, does not get to decide when the house is ready. His father does. The groom goes to get his bride when the father tells him the house is finished.

Jesus' promise is made not only to the disciples, but also to us whom He has saved. Jesus is the groom and His church is the bride. He has promised there are many places for all of us to live with Him in His Father's house. He has also promised to come back and take us home so we can be with Him. His death was the price he paid to make this happen. His resurrection guarantees it will happen.

How much more could He do to show us He wants us around?

We Are Redeemed

Redemption is something we all long for. We all have done things we wish we could go back and do over. A parent wasn't there in a critical situation when the child needed them. The parent is there the next time the situation occurs, so the parent is, therefore, redeemed by being there this time. Someone does something that hurts someone else and ends up ruining a relationship. We say the relationship is redeemed when the person goes and makes things right with the other person and the relationship is restored.

In these situations, and many others like them, redemption happens when we do something. Specifically when we do something that makes things right. We apologize for words said that hurt someone. We do community service for crimes we've committed. We go to rehab to overcome our addictions and start to live sober lives. These are just a few of the many ways we seek to redeem our lives and ourselves. We right the wrongs we've done in our lives and we feel redeemed.

The problem with seeing redemption this way is there is one thing we can't undo or make right. We can't make our sin right. We can't undo the way we've insulted a holy and perfect God by saying we know better than Him and we are going to do what we think is right, not what He says is right. We can't call God's character and goodness into question, apologize to Him by saying "my bad," and expect Him to overlook it the way we want Him to.

We've managed to turn our lives into lives of isolation, loneliness, pain, and futility. We've learned to live in guilt and shame, which is destroying us. While we may find periods of relief, especially in our addictions, we can't make this relief permanent. Hope is something that eludes us on a daily basis. We just can't find it when we want it.

There is a price to be paid for all of this. The price of redemption is so high that we can't pay it ourselves. God chose to pay this price, because of His great love for us, to remove the separation between us caused by our sin.

God chose to do this through the death of Jesus. He came to serve as the ransom, or payment, for many (Matthew 20:28). Romans 3:24 and Colossians 1:14 both teach redemption from sin is only found in Jesus. It is through the shed blood of Jesus that our sins are covered when we ask Jesus to save us (Ephesians 1:7).

God not only redeemed us from sin, but He also redeemed our lives. God accomplished this through Jesus' resurrection. One reason Jesus came was to give us a new life, a new way of living (John 10:10). God's desire is to redeem us from a life of futility, guilt, and shame. God desires we live the life of meaning, value, and dignity He intended.

We Are Restored

Now that God has redeemed us, He is able to restore His relationship with us. God is able to move toward us and restore, or re-establish, a relationship with each of us because the wall of sin between us is removed when we ask Jesus to save us. God's restoration of His relationship with us opens the door for us to experience the new life promised in John 10:10.

There are two things that are true about this new life. First, before Jesus saved us, we had only one way to live.

We lived without God and we lived self-centered lives. Romans 6:16 teaches that we were slaves to sin, which prevented us from living in relationship with God and finding the life He intended for us.

The second thing it teaches is we can live the new life promised in John 10:10, because we are now made new in Jesus. Those who asked Jesus to save them are no longer the same as they were before they were saved. God's relationship with us gives us all we need to live in allegiance with Him as Romans 6:16 also teaches us.

We don't have to live like slaves to sin anymore. We can choose to live our lives differently than we did in the past. We can choose to live lives which focus on others, not just ourselves. We can choose to live lives centered on God and what He wants for our lives because He has restored us to Himself. God has saved us from the Devil's domain and moved us under the rule and reign of Jesus (Colossians 1:13).

A New Way to See Life

God's restoration of His relationship with us allows us to learn to see the world, others, and ourselves as God does. We begin to see the brokenness around us. Yet we also become aware of the worth, value, and dignity God has given His creation and us.

An important part of this foundation is we are at peace with God because of what Jesus did through His death and resurrection. According to Colossians 2:13–14, God removed the hostility and alienation we have experienced because of our sin by placing our sin on Jesus and nailing it to the cross with Him. Jesus' shed blood covered our sins and brought peace to our relationship with God (Colossians 1:20). We can have peace with God because of our faith in Jesus (Romans 5:1).

It's important to point out that this peace between God and us is God's doing, not ours. It was God reaching out in love to us to make a way for our sins to be forgiven so that we can have peace with Him. God is the one who took the initiative to begin the restoration process, and He is the one who will bring it to completion when we die or when Jesus comes back, whichever occurs first.

An important part of the restoration of God's relationship with us is the restoration of God's image in each of us. He is restoring our hearts so that we can think, feel, and make choices based on who He really is and not the distorted picture we have of Him. He is restoring our ability and desire to pursue our relationship with Him by drawing us to Him.

God is working to restore how we represent Him in this world. He is working to restore our ability to be compassionate, to show mercy and grace, and to love more deeply. He is working to restore His image in us.

God wants us to see the world for what it is—broken. He wants us to see and feel the sin that destroys it. He wants us to see He still loves His creation, however, and one day He will renew it to what it should have been all along, as Romans 8:18–23 teaches. He wants us to see the hope that is ours in the midst of the world's brokenness.

God desires for us to see other people as they are—broken. We are all broken by sin. This is why we need to be restored by God. God deeply desires people to know He loves them and wants them to come to Him so He can save them and restore His relationship with them. He wants us to see them as people with needs not just as objects to be exploited.

God deeply desires that we acknowledge our own brokenness. He desires we acknowledge our need for Him. He longs for us to realize we can't handle life without Him.

He longs for His children to accept His love and forgiveness. He wants us to live free from guilt and shame. His desire is for us to see how much He loves us. He longs for us to draw near to Him (Hebrews 10:22).

The Gospel opens the door for us to live life as God intended us to. Pledging our allegiance to God as Lord and King allows us to live life with direction and purpose. His forgiveness helps us learn to live free from guilt and shame. In Him, we have a safe place to call home.

The Gospel also promises we aren't alone or without hope. In the next chapter we'll take a look at who is along for the ride with us on this journey and where we can find the hope we need so we don't give up.

Scripture References

Philippians 2:12–13

"So then, my beloved, just as you have always obeyed, not as in my presence only, but now much more in my absence, work out your salvation with fear and trembling; for it is God who is at work in you, both to will and to work for His good pleasure."

Ephesians 2:10
"For we are His workmanship, created in Christ Jesus for good works, which God prepared beforehand so that we would walk in them."

1 Corinthians 12:4–6
"Now there are varieties of gifts, but the same Spirit. And there are varieties of ministries, and the same Lord. There are varieties of effects, but the same God who works all things in all persons."

Matthew 28:19-20
"Go therefore and make disciples of all the nations, baptizing them in the name of the Father and the Son and the Holy Spirit, teaching them to observe all that I commanded you; and lo, I am with you always, even to the end of the age."

Genesis 50:20
"As for you, you meant evil against me, but God meant it for good in order to bring about this present result, to preserve many people alive."

Romans 8:28–29
"And we know that God causes all things to work together for good to those who love God, to those who are called according to *His* purpose. For those whom He foreknew, He also predestined *to become* conformed to the image of His Son, so that He would be the firstborn among many brethren."

Philippians 1:6
"For I am confident of this very thing, that He who began a good work in you will perfect it until the day of Christ Jesus."

Hebrews 8:12
"For I will be merciful to their iniquities, And I will remember their sins no more."

Hebrews 10:17
"And their sins and their lawless deeds I will remember no more."

Jeremiah 31:31–34
"Behold, days are coming," declares the Lord,

"when I will make a new covenant with the house of Israel and with the house of Judah, not like the covenant which I made with their fathers in the day I took them by the hand to bring them out of the land of Egypt, My covenant which they broke, although I was a husband to them," declares the Lord. "But this is the covenant which I will make with the house of Israel after those days," declares the Lord, "I will put My law within them and on their heart I will write it; and I will be their God, and they shall be My people. "They will not teach again, each man his neighbor and each man his brother, saying, 'Know the Lord,' for they will all know Me, from the least of them to the greatest of them," declares the Lord, "for I will forgive their iniquity, and their sin I will remember no more."

Psalm 103:8–12
"The Lord is compassionate and gracious,
Slow to anger and abounding in lovingkindness.
He will not always strive with us,
Nor will He keep His anger forever.
He has not dealt with us according to our sins,
Nor rewarded us according to our iniquities.
For as high as the heavens are above the earth,
So great is His lovingkindness toward those who
 fear Him.
As far as the east is from the west,
So far has He removed our transgressions from us."

Isaiah 43:25
"I, even I, am the one who wipes out your transgressions for My own sake, And I will not remember your sins."

1 John 1:9
"If we confess our sins, He is faithful and righteous to forgive us our sins and to cleanse us from all unrighteousness."

Revelation 22:13
"I am the Alpha and the Omega, the first and the last, the beginning and the end."

Psalm 51:3–4
"For I know my transgressions,
And my sin is ever before me.
Against You, You only, I have sinned
And done what is evil in Your sight,
So that You are justified when You speak
And blameless when You judge."

Romans 8:15–16
"For you have not received a spirit of slavery leading to fear again, but you have received a spirit of adoption as sons by which we cry out, 'Abba! Father!' The Spirit Himself testifies with our spirit that we are children of God."

John 3:16–17
"For God so loved the world, that He gave His only begotten Son, that whoever believes in Him shall not perish, but have eternal life. For God did not send the Son into the world to judge the world, but that the world might be saved through Him."

Romans 7:13–25
"Therefore did that which is good become a cause of death for me? May it never be! Rather it was sin, in order that it might be shown to be sin by effecting my death through that which is good, so that through the commandment sin would become utterly sinful. For we know that the Law is spiritual, but I am of flesh, sold into bondage to sin. For what I am doing, I do not understand; for I am not practicing what I would like to do, but I am doing the very thing I hate. But if I do the very thing I do not want to do, I agree with the Law, confessing that the Law is good. So now, no longer am I the one

doing it, but sin, which dwells in me. For I know that nothing good dwells in me, that is, in my flesh; for the willing is present in me, but the doing of the good is not. For the good that I want, I do not do, but I practice the very evil that I do not want. But if I am doing the very thing I do not want, I am no longer the one doing it, but sin which dwells in me. I find, then, the principle that evil is present in me, the one who wants to do good. For I joyfully concur with the law of God in the inner man, but I see a different law in the members of my body, waging war against the law of my mind and making me a prisoner of the law of sin which is in my members. Wretched man that I am! Who will set me free from the body of this death? Thanks be to God through Jesus Christ our Lord! So then, on the one hand I myself with my mind am serving the law of God, but on the other, with my flesh the law of sin."

James 4:17
"Therefore, to one who knows the right thing to do and does not do it, to him it is sin."

Romans 7:24–25
"Wretched man that I am! Who will set me free from the body of this death? Thanks be to God through Jesus Christ our Lord! So then, on the

one hand I myself with my mind am serving the law of God, but on the other, with my flesh the law of sin."

Romans 8:1

"Therefore there is now no condemnation for those who are in Christ Jesus."

Romans 8:33–34

"Who will bring a charge against God's elect? God is the one who justifies; who is the one who condemns? Christ Jesus is He who died, yes, rather who was raised, who is at the right hand of God, who also intercedes for us."

Romans 15:7

"Therefore, accept one another, just as Christ also accepted us to the glory of God."

Colossians 3:9–11

"You laid aside the old self with its evil practices, and have put on the new self who is being renewed to a true knowledge according to the image of the One who created him—a renewal in which there is no distinction between Greek and Jew, circumcised and uncircumcised, barbarian, Scythian, slave and freeman, but Christ is all, and in all."

Luke 15:10
"In the same way, I tell you, there is joy in the presence of the angels of God over one sinner who repents."

Jeremiah 24:7
'I will give them a heart to know Me, for I am the Lord; and they will be My people, and I will be their God, for they will return to Me with their whole heart."

John 14:1–3
"Do not let your heart be troubled; believe in God, believe also in Me. In My Father's house are many dwelling places; if it were not so, I would have told you; for I go to prepare a place for you. If I go and prepare a place for you, I will come again and receive you to Myself, that where I am, there you may be also."

Matthew 20:28
". . . just as the Son of Man did not come to be served, but to serve, and to give His life a ransom for many."

Ephesians 1:7
"In Him we have redemption through His blood, the forgiveness of our trespasses, according to the riches of His grace."

Romans 3:23-24
"For all have sinned and fall short of the glory of God, being justified as a gift by His grace through the redemption which is in Christ Jesus."

Colossians 1:13-14
"For He rescued us from the domain of darkness, and transferred us to the kingdom of His beloved Son, in whom we have redemption, the forgiveness of sins."

John 10:10

"The thief comes only to steal and kill and destroy; I came that they may have life, and have it abundantly."

Romans 6:16

"Do you not know that when you present yourselves to someone as slaves for obedience, you are slaves of the one whom you obey, either of sin resulting in death, or of obedience resulting in righteousness?"

Colossians 1:13

"For He rescued us from the domain of darkness, and transferred us to the kingdom of His beloved Son."

Colossians 2:13–14

"When you were dead in your transgressions and the uncircumcision of your flesh, He made you alive together with Him, having forgiven us all our transgressions, having canceled out the certificate of debt consisting of decrees against us, which was hostile to us; and He has taken it out of the way, having nailed it to the cross."

Colossians 1:19–20
"For it was the Father's good pleasure for
all the fullness to dwell in Him, and through
Him to reconcile all things to Himself, having
made peace through the blood of His cross;
through Him, I say, whether things on earth or
things in heaven."

Romans 5:1
"Therefore, having been justified by faith, we have
peace with God through our Lord Jesus
Christ."

Romans 8:18–23
"For I consider that the sufferings of this present
time are not worthy to be compared with the
glory that is to be revealed to us. For the
anxious longing of the creation waits eagerly
for the revealing of the sons of God. For the
creation was subjected to futility, not willingly,
but because of Him who subjected it, in hope
that the creation itself also will be set free from
its slavery to corruption into the freedom of the
glory of the children of God. For we know that
the whole creation groans and suffers the pains
of childbirth together until now. And not only
this, but also we ourselves, having the first fruits
of the Spirit, even we ourselves groan within

ourselves, waiting eagerly for our adoption as sons, the redemption of our body."

Hebrews 10:22
"Let us draw near with a sincere heart in full assurance of faith, having our hearts sprinkled clean from an evil conscience and our bodies washed with pure water."

7

WHO'S WITH ME?

Knowing who is with you is more important than knowing where you're going.
—Steven Furtick

Just remaining quietly in the presence of God, listening to Him, being attentive to Him, requires a lot of courage and know-how.
—Thomas Merton

It's important to understand that when we ask Jesus to save us, God's relationship with us is restored. This means we are no longer alienated from God, but are now part of his family as, Romans 8:15–17 points out. We are now sons and daughters of God.

In the last chapter we looked at three of the six most

important truths that become true of us when we ask Jesus to save us. These three truths, God becomes Lord and King in our lives, we're forgiven, and we have a place to belong to are important building blocks for the foundation of God's relationship with us.

In this chapter, we will look at the other three truths that become true of us when we ask Jesus to save us. In all, these six truths work together to form a solid foundation for God's relationship with us. We need to know we're not alone on this journey, God loves us unconditionally, and we can find hope in this relationship.

We Are Not Alone

Loneliness is something we've all felt. We've all had the feeling no one is there is for us. We learn to believe no one has our backs, no one cares about us, or no one wants us around. We feel humiliated by those we call "friends." Our guilt and shame become so heavy we believe we deserve to be alone.

Loneliness has been a constant companion of mine. Looking back over my life, it was easy to for me to feel alone. I've struggled with believing people wanted me around simply for who I was. I was an easy target for others to bully and humiliate growing up. I started to believe I didn't fit in anywhere, especially at church and home.

I've struggled with not feeling good enough. Performing became my main way of coping with it. If anyone wanted something done, they knew to come find me because I'd do it. Eventually, even this didn't give me the acceptance I craved. I still felt a deep loneliness I couldn't shake.

My loneliness led me to my addictions. I thought my

addictions offered me an answer to my loneliness. My addictions offered me a safe place to live. They didn't demand I be good enough. I found freedom from being judged and a place I was accepted. My addictions never rejected me. My addictions became my best friends.

Over time, my addictions went from being my best friends to being my worst enemies. Instead of being a safe place, they became a prison I couldn't escape from. I used relationships to keep people at a distance. I couldn't let others in for fear they'd reject me if they really knew me. I began to live in a self-imposed isolation I couldn't escape. My addictions only made my loneliness worse.

I left many people hurt and confused. They couldn't understand why I chose to live the way I did. Many would have accepted me as I was, but I couldn't accept myself. I didn't believe I was good enough for anyone. My addictions got in the way of me finding the life I longed for.

I chose to continue living this way even after I became a Christian. Now I had a new group of people I believed I couldn't be good enough for. I also had a God I couldn't be good enough for. I felt the judgment of others in a new and deeper way. I couldn't find what I longed for from my addictions or from others. It seemed my life was destined to be a story filled with loneliness and isolation.

The Gospel, however, offers a different story, one filled with the things I crave, such as a new relationship that doesn't demand I be good enough. The Gospel offers the story of love, acceptance, and forgiveness I have longed for. And finally, it offers me a story of freedom from the chains of my addictions and the guilt and shame that come from them.

God didn't create us to live in loneliness and isolation, but in relationship with Him, others, and ourselves. The

Gospel promises I don't have to live life alone and in isolation anymore. I can find the story, the life, I've longed to live in. The Gospel promises you can too.

God Is with Us

The Gospel promises God will be with us when we accept His offer of salvation in Jesus. I've struggled with this almost as much as I struggle with His grace and mercy. It's hard for me to understand how God knows everything about me—everything I say and do, and all my thoughts—and still say He loves me and wants me to be His companion in life? How can God say I'm a work of art in His eyes and He wants me to walk with Him? (Psalm 139:1–14). How can God say that about any of us?

Studying the Gospel has given me the answers to my questions. The Gospel continually reminds me that He has forgiven all my sins—past, present and future. The wall between God and me has been permanently removed through Jesus. God has "put his money where His mouth is" to make it possible for us to walk through life together. I feel humbled and overwhelmed knowing what God has done to make this happen. Knowing nothing can separate me from Him is comforting and gives me a great sense of security during the hard times. The same is true for anyone who asks Jesus to save them.

God's presence in our lives promises us several things. First, God's presence promises our lives have purpose and meaning. God's purpose for us may seem hard to find, but His presence in our lives guarantees we will accomplish His purpose for our lives. God's presence in our lives guarantees we have a valuable and meaningful life to live.

I find hope for my future in God's presence in my life. I

now have hope for a life that matters because Ephesians 2:10 tells me God has things He wants to accomplish through me. God won't quit working in my life until He accomplishes His purpose for me (Philippians 2:13). This means I have hope that I won't miss what He wants to accomplish in me and through me, because He is the one who will accomplish it. He has given me the skills and gifts to accomplish His purposes for my life (1 Corinthians 12:4–7).

Second, God isn't oblivious to what's going on in my life. God never promised a life free from pain and suffering. Instead, God promises to walk through it with me and to bring good out of it. Romans 8:28 is God's promise to do this for all who are saved by Jesus, just as God did for Joseph in Genesis 50:20. God's presence in my life means all the pain and suffering I've experienced isn't the final word on my life.

Third, God's presence in my life is bringing healing and freedom. God has used the pain and suffering in my life to change me from the inside out. I'm learning how to forgive others and that forgiveness doesn't let the other person off the hook, Instead, it frees me to live the life God wants me to live.

God is changing me into a man who can empathize with others instead of judging them. I'm beginning to look through peoples' actions and into their hearts because of God's presence. I'm finding my purpose for my life because of God's presence in my life. The promise of the Gospel is God will do the same for all who come to Jesus to be saved.

Jesus Is with Us

Jesus loved us so much, He was willing to come and pay the price for our sins. How amazing is that? Jesus, God the Son and the second member of the Trinity, chose to leave heaven, give up His right to use His privileges as God, became like us, and went through the excruciating pain of the crucifixion so we can have our sins forgiven. Then He told death to take a hike, rose from the dead, and now sits at the right hand of God the Father.

I find it hard to believe Jesus did all this just to experience life as we do. He did it so He could experience the pressures of life we experience. Jesus willingly chose to experience the homelessness, poverty, and racism many of us experience. Jesus experienced the hatred and condemnation of those who should have welcomed Him with open arms.

Jesus willingly chose to be human. He chose to experience the same pain, heartache, and hurt we experience. He understands what it's like to be betrayed and abandoned by those He knows and loves. Jesus knows what it feels like to be lonely, abused, beaten, publicly humiliated, hated, and ignored by those who should have honored him.

This is why I find comfort in Hebrews 2:17–18 and 4:15–16. Jesus came and suffered the same things all us have suffered. Jesus knows what it takes to live in this world and is able to help me live the life God desires me to live. Jesus offers the mercy and grace I need to continue on my journey of life.

All of this gives Jesus' promise to be with us and to live within us an even deeper meaning. Jesus understands what we go through in life. He is able to empathize with us in the midst of our pain and suffering and offer us comfort and security like no one else can. Jesus is able to touch us at our deepest level.

I don't know how many times I've had well-meaning individuals downplay or try to minimize my life experiences. Every person who suffers from addiction has heard "Just get over it" or "Why can't you just stop" over and over again. I had one pastor ask me why I can't just grab hold of the truth, forget the past, and move on. I laughed at it, but deep down it hurt me deeply. I've found many people have a hard time empathizing with what I've experienced, and continue to experience, in my life.

But, I've found Jesus doesn't do this. Jesus doesn't downplay, minimize, or dismiss our life experiences. Instead, He gives a sense of honor and dignity to our lives when he chose to become human and experience life as we do. Jesus "gets it."

Jesus' presence in our lives also means He is with us in our lowest moments. We may not understand why things happen to us or why we do the things we do, but Jesus promises to be with us through it all. He understands the hurt, pain, and suffering we go through because He's lived it too.

Jesus becoming human validates my worth. It means Jesus walks with me, values me, and cares enough to want to be part of my life. It means I'm loved and wanted. Jesus' presence with me means my life matters.

Jesus' presence also helps me experience a peace I can't explain as I draw near to Him. Jesus is alive and walks with me in the loneliest and most painful places of my life, including my addictions. With His help, I can deal with the disappointments of life. It means I'm not alone in life.

Most of all, Jesus desires to be in my life so much that He gave up everything to make it possible. He died in order to be present in my life. I am worth dying for, and so are you.

The Holy Spirit Is with Us

I think the Holy Spirit is the hardest member of the Trinity for me to relate to. I can relate to God the Father because I can see His power and beauty when I see the mountains or look at the ocean. I can relate to Jesus, God the Son, because He lived and walked as a human. But, the Holy Spirit is different.

I see the work of God the Father in the world around me. I look at the cross and the empty tomb to see what Jesus, God the Son, has done for me. But, I need to look to the past to see the work the Holy Spirit, God the Spirit, has done in my life. I only see the changes the Holy Spirit has made in me, and others, after the work has been completed.

However, it's important to understand the role the Holy Spirit plays in the lives of those saved by Jesus. We experience the presence of God and Jesus in our lives through the Holy Spirit, who lives in us, teaches us, brings us comfort, and points us to Jesus (John 14:16–17, 26–27, 15:26; John 16:13–14).

The Holy Spirit's presence in us is God's guarantee of, or down payment for, our salvation. The Spirit is God's "seal of approval" on all who ask Jesus to save them. The Holy Spirit in us is God's promise we are now His and one day our salvation will be made complete when Jesus returns. I find great comfort and security in Ephesians 1:13–14 and 2 Corinthians 1:21–22, which testify to this good news.

The Spirit's presence means I'm a child of God and a member of His family. I know God won't disown me or kick me out of the family because of my sin. I can rely on God's promise to forgive my sins—past, present, and future. I no longer have to live with the guilt and shame I've carried for so long (Romans 8:1–2; 33–34).

The Holy Spirit is with me on my journey through life teaching me, guiding me, convicting me, and changing me from the inside out. The Holy Spirit is my constant companion on this road of life, even in my darkest moments.

A Personal Side Note

My relationship with the Holy Spirit hasn't always been great. For many years I gave lip service to the Holy Spirit's presence in my life. Too often I've been a hypocrite, judging others for the same things I was doing. I couldn't look at myself because I couldn't stop doing the things I knew were sinful and wrong. I couldn't understand or figure out why I couldn't change.

I had to come to the end of myself, hit rock bottom if you will, to realize I couldn't stop on my own. I needed help. I found the only One who could give me the help I needed is the Holy Spirit.

Also, I realized I am not God, yet I tried to live like I was. I tried to control everything and everyone in my life to make sure I was safe and happy. I said, "See, I don't need You. I can do it on my own." When I finally got honest with myself, I had to admit I couldn't do it on my own. My life was in shambles.

I needed help to put it back together. Enter the Holy Spirit. I realized the Holy Spirit was the only one who could help me deal with my denial that I needed God. The Holy Spirit is the only one who can reach deep enough into my heart to shine a light on it and then start to change it. I surrendered and gave the Holy Spirit permission to change me. I repented from trying to run my own life and asked the Holy Spirit to run it. It has been a wild roller coaster ever since.

My life, including my past, has a purpose and meaning it never had before. My past is no longer a ball and chain. I'm using my past as a tool to understand others and to help them to find the freedom I've found. Heck, even this book is a result of this.

I don't have all the answers and it's okay. The Holy Spirit is able to teach me what I don't know. The Spirit is able to reveal and develop the gifts, skills, and strengths I've been given. I bring more to the table than I ever knew I could.

The Holy Spirit is leading me into a new life by teaching me how to use my gifts and skills to make a positive impact in others' lives and to build better relationships. How I choose to live my life does matter. My life has significance and is essential to those around me. I count.

The Spirit is teaching me I am not my addiction. I'm not a slave to my addictions anymore. The Holy Spirit inside of me gives me the strength I need to say no to my addictions. I'm now living as a man who has addictions instead of someone who suffers from addiction. All this is possible thanks to the Holy Spirit living inside of me.

I used to wonder what the Holy Spirit was doing in my life because I couldn't feel or see what the Spirit was doing. Now I not only have a better understanding what the Spirit has been doing, but I realize the Holy Spirit has done more in my life than I ever imagined.

We Become Part of the Church

We become part of the church when we are saved. The church can be polarizing. Some have been hurt deeply by it. Others have been helped deeply by it. Some see it as being irrelevant and unnecessary. Yet, no matter how we experience or see it, all who are saved by Jesus are part of it.

I admit that the church is not perfect. The church has developed a reputation of shooting its wounded rather than offering a safe place for those hurting to come in and find help. The church can be very judgmental and not empathetic. My experience of church for many years was severe judgment and lack of empathy for my pain.

I also admit I was part of the problem. I judged others harshly because I wasn't willing to face the problems in myself that I was judging them for. On one hand, I wanted everyone else to show me the grace and mercy I needed. But on the other, I was unwilling to show others the same thing. It made for a miserable life of guilt, shame, confusion, and loneliness.

Yet the church is still the body of Christ. All Christians are part of it. The question is, what do we want to make it? Do we want it to be a place of healing and hope, or do we want it to be a place of judgment and shame? As men and women who suffer from addictions, we have the opportunity to make the church a place where we can find the hope and healing we long for.

It took me a long time to realize that I had to admit my addictions before I could become part of the answer to the problem I saw within the church I attended. I learned it wasn't okay for the men and women who suffer from addictions to be looked at as outsiders and to be forgotten.

The Holy Spirit gave me a new purpose for my life as

the Spirit continued to rebuild me from the inside out. I began to see the church doesn't hate those with addictions. The church simply doesn't understand addiction—how it works or what causes it. I had a pastor once ask me, "How long are you going to struggle? Just believe the truth and move on." I laughed it off, but deep down it hurt. He didn't understand what I was going through. I had another pastor at the same church tell me he wanted to know what I wanted him to pray for, but he didn't want to know the details behind my requests. I felt like he wanted to do his "duty" and pray for me, but he didn't want to get his hands dirty and help me struggle through what was going on in my life. He wanted to play it safe. He wanted to pray for me but not get involved in my life.

The local church is the place where we build our new life in Christ, but I wasn't finding it to be a safe place to do this. Few in the church could help me identify the gifts and skills the Holy Spirit was trying to develop in me, because most people couldn't relate to me. I was "different." They were unable to teach me how to live in freedom from the guilt and shame of my past so I could live this new life. My guilt and shame seemed to intensify and strengthen the more I went to church. I felt even more worthless, less valued, and had less dignity.

This was my experience for many years. Yet God never quit pursuing me and drawing me to Him. During this time, the Holy Spirit taught me a lesson I will never forget. I learned that when I point my finger at someone, I have three pointing back at me. I realized I was part of the problem in the church. I also learned if I'm part of the problem, then I can be part of the solution.

This is why I believe those of us who suffer from addictions are needed in the church today. We are able to change the way the church looks at men and women who suffer from addictions by getting directly involved in a local church. We can educate the church about addiction, how it impacts everyone in the congregation. By being aware of our needs and the needs of those we have hurt, the church can bring a new sense of hope to those who suffer from addiction. As a result, we can break down barriers to offer the support, encouragement, compassion, and empathy we all need to not only survive, but thrive. We can make the church a safe place to heal and find the freedom we all long for.

I went to Denver Seminary in 2006 and started working on my master's in counseling. During the five years I spent working toward the degree, the Holy Spirit started working in me to show me my addictions and the impact they were having in my life. I found a local church that became a safe place for me to work on healing my addictions. The church has helped me discover and use my God-given gifts to build up myself and others, as Ephesians 4:1–3, 10–16, and 1 Corinthians 12:4–7 teach us to do. I have felt the burden of my guilt and shame being lifted since attending this church. The pastors are open to hearing how their messages impact those who suffer from addiction and are willing to adjust accordingly.

This church gave me the acceptance I craved as it ministered to me, as Ephesians 4:1–3 and Romans 15:7 teaches the church to do. I am treated with the worth, dignity, and value I was created with. I've found the encouragement I need to keep going as I made Hebrews 10:24–25 a reality. I have seen and experienced how forgiveness, redemption, and restoration can change someone's life. I've learned my life counts. If I can a find church like this, so can you.

We Are Loved Unconditionally

We all long to be loved unconditionally. Yet being loved unconditionally is something we rarely experience. We struggle in our relationships to be loved for who we are. It's a struggle we can't win.

One reason we can't win this struggle is based on how we define what love means. Society teaches us love is based on our emotions. That it's based on how people make us feel. Love is love only when someone meets our expectations. We think, *I will love you if, or because, you make me feel good.* Or, *If you love me, you'll do what I want.* Our definition of love becomes based on how the other person makes us feel or what they will do for us rather than who the other person is. When they quit meeting our expectations, the love goes away. We "fall out of love" with the person.

This definition of love made sense to me growing up and influenced my life in many ways. First, my life was centered on finding someone who could say they loved me. It became all I lived for. I became "addicted" to finding love. Second, this definition taught me I wasn't worth loving. Many times what I thought was love ended up with me being used instead of being loved. Sometimes I smothered the other person, which pushed them away. Third, this contradiction between wanting desperately to be loved and not feeling worthy of it left me in a constant state of despair and depression. Fourth, it prevented me from finding the only love that could give me what I longed for—unconditional love. It blinded me to the love God offers to all of us.

Fortunately, God's love isn't based on what we do. He knows everything about us. God knows we don't measure up to His standard of perfection. He knows the "skeletons in our closets." And yet God still chooses to love us. God's love for us is unconditional.

This is what makes what God chose to do through Jesus so amazing to me. God's love is something we can't earn, be good enough for, or deserve because of our sin. Yet He loves us and was willing to sacrifice Jesus to pay the price for our sins to demonstrate His love for us.

Studying the Gospel has opened my eyes to what real unconditional love is. God's definition of unconditional love isn't based on our performance. God's unconditional love isn't based on sentimental feelings or fluctuating emotions. God's unconditional love for us is based on who He is and the fact that He created us in His image. It's the reason God sent Jesus to restore and redeem His relationship with us.

God's unconditional love is active, not passive. It's the foundation for what He does in our lives to deepen His relationship with us. It is why God works in our lives to enable us to know what His will for us is and to motivate us to live it out (Philippians 2:13).

We are who we are in Jesus because of God's unconditional love. I love Romans 15:7 because the verse points out we are unconditionally accepted by God. I also gain hope from Romans 8:1–2 and Colossians 2:13–14 because my sins have been forgiven and are not counted against me. Guilt and shame no longer have a hold on me. God calls me His child and friend in Galatians 4:5–7 and John 15:13–14.

The new and abundant life promised in John 10:10 is becoming a reality for me because of God's unconditional love. I'm able to live a new life without guilt and shame. Fear, which has dominated my life, is losing its foothold.

Old ways of protecting myself are giving way to being able to trust God and others.

My life is often chaotic and difficult. Sometimes it's painful and has its share of suffering. God never promised my life would free from these things as long as I live in this broken world. The one thing I can count on is that I will always be loved and will never be alone, because His unconditional love for me will never change. This gives me the security to face life and God can do the same for you if you ask Him.

We Have Hope

Understanding I'm not alone on this journey and I'm loved unconditionally has given me one other thing the Gospel promises. That is the promise of hope. Hope is critical to our lives. We can't live without hope. Proverbs 13:12 and 17:22 remind us that life is not easy to live without hope. It's easy to give up and quit on life without it.

Sometimes hope was the only thing keeping me going. There were several times, in my twenties, that I considered killing myself. Life seemed hopeless. I couldn't stand who I had become, and I felt alone and isolated. I had just spent five years working on a master's degree that I didn't finish but told everyone I was going to. I was working as a janitor cleaning up operating rooms after surgeries at a local hospital. I was living with a lot of shame and guilt. Life sucked.

One thing kept me going: hope. Hope that there was more to life. Hope that I could move on and find the life I longed for. Hope that I would find the love and relationships I desperately wanted. I found this hope, not in people or things, but in the Gospel.

I found hope is only as strong as the object we put it in.

I placed my hope for finding the love and acceptance I craved in others, my job on campus, being in school, and being around those I thought loved me. I looked for validation and significance in my friends, my church, and the campus ministry I was involved in. They all let me down. They couldn't give me what I wanted. They were incapable of doing what I was asking them to do.

Finally, I turned to my addictions. I put my hope in them to help get through life. I hoped they could relieve the frustration with the way my life was going. I hoped they would give me a sense of control and power, which I thought would help me feel more like the man everyone told me I should be.

They did what I hoped for—temporarily. I felt what I wanted to when I engaged in my addictions. The problem was when I quit I felt worse than I did before. I went through the cycle all of us who suffer from addictions feel. I engaged with my addictions because they made me feel better, but afterward the guilt and shame would be so heavy I'd engage in my addictions again to feel better. It seemed like a never-ending downward spiral I couldn't get out of.

This went on for twenty years into my forties. The year I graduated from Denver Seminary I started working in a detox facility. I started to see firsthand how addictions impacted peoples' lives, including mine. I studied the Gospel to see how it could impact addictions and bring change to those who suffer. In doing so, I found the Gospel offers more hope for change than I realized.

The Gospel offers hope based on God's unconditional love, not on people, things, or circumstances. This hope is based on the promises God has made to us in the Gospel—

now and in the future. And as Romans 5:5 tells us, this hope won't disappoint us.

The Gospel offers hope for a new life and a new way of living today. It promises we don't have to live as slaves to our addictions. The Gospel promises freedom from the guilt and shame we've slaved under because of our past. It promises God will bring something good out of our past. Nothing we've done or experienced will be wasted. The Gospel offers the hope for a new life and a better future.

God promises we won't remain the same. He will bring about changes in us so we start to reflect who Jesus is. We will become "new creations," as 2 Corinthians 5:17 tells us, as we learn to live out the new ways of living He has promised us and leave the old ways behind.

We are promised a new relationship with God through Jesus. Our new relationship guarantees our lives will be full of meaning and purpose. God promises we will be coworkers with Him to bring about His plan for humanity and history. He will provide the gifts and skills we need to carry out our part in His plan for humanity. The image of God within each of us is restored, and our inherent worth, value, and dignity is confirmed by Jesus' death and resurrection.

The Gospel also includes a promise of hope for the future. God promises this life is not the last word on our lives. He promises Jesus will come back and judge this world. The curse of sin will be removed, and all creation will be renewed. This world will become what it was meant to be when it was created; a place of no tears, pain, sorrow, or death. It will be perfect, and so will all those who ask Jesus to save them.

I must admit there were many times I lost hope and gave up on finding the life I wanted. I watched as others found what I thought I wanted, but I couldn't. I came to the conclusion I wasn't worthy of having anything I wanted in life. I was being punished for all the things I ever did.

Studying the Gospel has proved to me I was wrong. I found my hope being restored as I read verses like Romans 8:38–39, John 14:1–3, and Romans 15:7, which tell me I am loved, wanted, and accepted when I thought I wasn't. 2 Corinthians 5:14–17, Colossians 3:9–10, and Philippians 2:13 give me the hope I can change. I can live a new life. I believed I was worthless until I started to believe Ephesians 2:10 is true. I thought I was destined to live with the guilt and shame of my past. But I found out I didn't have to as I meditated on Romans 8:1–2 and 1 John 1:9.

The Gospel has restored my hope in the promises of God. I can't wait for my hope to become reality when everything will be made new and the pain, heartache, and suffering of this world will be undone as Revelation 21:1–6 teaches. In that day, I will finally be perfect, without sin, and restored. I will finally be who I was created to be. So can you, if you ask.

Scripture References

Romans 8:15–17
"For you have not received a spirit of slavery leading to fear again, but you have received a spirit of adoption as sons by which we cry out, 'Abba! Father!' The Spirit Himself testifies with our spirit that we are children of God, and if children, heirs also, heirs of God and fellow

heirs with Christ, if indeed we suffer with Him so that we may also be glorified with Him."

John 17:20–21

"I do not ask on behalf of these alone, but for those
    also who believe in Me through their word;
that they may all be one; even as You, Father, are in
    Me and I in You, that they also may be in Us, so
    that the world may believe that You sent Me."

Psalm 139:1–14

O Lord, You have searched me and known me.
You know when I sit down and when I rise up;
You understand my thought from afar.
You scrutinize my path and my lying down,
And are intimately acquainted with all my ways.
Even before there is a word on my tongue,
Behold, O Lord, You know it all.
You have enclosed me behind and before,
And laid Your hand upon me.
Such knowledge is too wonderful for me;
It is too high, I cannot attain to it.
Where can I go from Your Spirit?
Or where can I flee from Your presence?
If I ascend to heaven, You are there;
If I make my bed in Sheol, behold, You are there.
If I take the wings of the dawn,
If I dwell in the remotest part of the sea,
Even there Your hand will lead me,

And Your right hand will lay hold of me.
If I say, "Surely the darkness will overwhelm me,
And the light around me will be night,"
Even the darkness is not dark to You,
And the night is as bright as the day.
Darkness and light are alike to You.
For You formed my inward parts;
You wove me in my mother's womb.
I will give thanks to You, for I am fearfully and
   wonderfully made;
Wonderful are Your works,
And my soul knows it very well.

Ephesians 2:10
"For we are His workmanship, created in Christ
   Jesus for good works, which God prepared
   beforehand so that we would walk in them."

Philippians 2:13
"For it is God who is at work in you, both to will
   and to work for His good pleasure."

1 Corinthians 12:4–7
"Now there are varieties of gifts, but the same
   Spirit. And there are varieties of ministries, and
   the same Lord. There are varieties of effects,
   but the same God who works all things in all

persons. But to each one is given the manifestation of the Spirit for the common good."

Romans 8:28
"And we know that God causes all things to work together for good to those who love God, to those who are called according to His purpose."

Genesis 50:20
"As for you, you meant evil against me, but God meant it for good in order to bring about this present result, to preserve many people alive."

Hebrews 4:15–16
"For we do not have a high priest who cannot sympathize with our weaknesses, but One who has been tempted in all things as we are, yet without sin. Therefore let us draw near with confidence to the throne of grace, so that we may receive mercy and find grace to help in time of need."

Hebrews 2:17–18
"Therefore, He had to be made like His brethren in

all things, so that He might become a merciful and faithful high priest in things pertaining to God, to make propitiation for the sins of the people. For since He Himself was tempted in that which He has suffered, He is able to come to the aid of those who are tempted."

John 14:16–17

"I will ask the Father, and He will give you another Helper, that He may be with you forever; that is the Spirit of truth, whom the world cannot receive, because it does not see Him or know Him, but you know Him because He abides with you and will be in you."

John 14:26

"But the Helper, the Holy Spirit, whom the Father will send in My name, He will teach you all things, and bring to your remembrance all that I said to you."

Ephesians 1:13–14

"In Him, you also, after listening to the message of truth, the gospel of your salvation—having also believed, you were sealed in Him with the Holy Spirit of promise, who is given as a pledge of our inheritance, with a view to the redemption of God's own possession, to the praise of His glory."

2 Corinthians 1:21–22
"Now He who establishes us with you in Christ and anointed us is God, who also sealed us and gave us the Spirit in our hearts as a pledge."

Romans 8:1–2
"Therefore there is now no condemnation for those who are in Christ Jesus. For the law of the Spirit of life in Christ Jesus has set you free from the law of sin and of death."

Romans 8:33–34
"Who will bring a charge against God's elect? God is the one who justifies; who is the one who condemns? Christ Jesus is He who died, yes, rather who was raised, who is at the right hand of God, who also intercedes for us."

Ephesians 4:1–3
"Therefore I, the prisoner of the Lord, implore you to walk in a manner worthy of the calling with which you have been called, with all humility

and gentleness, with patience, showing tolerance for one another in love, being diligent to preserve the unity of the Spirit in the bond of peace."

Ephesians 4:10–16

"He who descended is Himself also He who ascended far above all the heavens, so that He might fill all things. And He gave some as apostles, and some as prophets, and some as evangelists, and some as pastors and teachers, for the equipping of the saints for the work of service, to the building up of the body of Christ; until we all attain to the unity of the faith, and of the knowledge of the Son of God, to a mature man, to the measure of the stature which belongs to the fullness of Christ. As a result, we are no longer to be children, tossed here and there by waves and carried about by every wind of doctrine, by the trickery of men, by craftiness in deceitful scheming; but speaking the truth in love, we are to grow up in all aspects into Him who is the head, even Christ, from whom the whole body, being fitted and held together by what every joint supplies, according to the proper working of each individual part, causes the growth of the body for the building up of itself in love."

1 Corinthians 12:4–7

"Now there are varieties of gifts, but the same Spirit. And there are varieties of ministries, and the same Lord. There are varieties of effects, but the same God who works all things in all persons. But to each one is given the manifestation of the Spirit for the common good."

Romans 8:1–2

"Therefore there is now no condemnation for those who are in Christ Jesus. For the law of the Spirit of life in Christ Jesus has set you free from the law of sin and of death."

Colossians 2:13–14

"When you were dead in your transgressions and the uncircumcision of your flesh, He made you alive together with Him, having forgiven us all our transgressions, having canceled out the certificate of debt consisting of decrees against us, which was hostile to us; and He has taken it out of the way, having nailed it to the cross."

John 15:13–14
"Greater love has no one than this, that one lay down his life for his friends. You are My friends if you do what I command you."

Galatians 4:4–7
"God sent forth His Son. . . . so that He might redeem those who were under the Law, that we might receive the adoption as sons. Because you are sons, God has sent forth the Spirit of His Son into our hearts, crying, "Abba! Father!" Therefore you are no longer a slave, but a son; and if a son, then an heir through God."

John 10:10
"The thief comes only to steal and kill and destroy; I came that they may have life, and have it abundantly."

Proverbs 13:12
"Hope deferred makes the heart sick,
But desire fulfilled is a tree of life."

Proverbs 17:22

"A joyful heart is good medicine,
But a broken spirit dries up the bones."

Romans 8:38–39

"For I am convinced that neither death, nor life, nor angels, nor principalities, nor things present, nor things to come, nor powers, nor height, nor depth, nor any other created thing, will be able to separate us from the love of God, which is in Christ Jesus our Lord."

Romans 15:7

"Therefore, accept one another, just as Christ also accepted us to the glory of God."

John 14:1–3

"Do not let your heart be troubled; believe in God, believe also in Me. In My Father's house are many dwelling places; if it were not so, I would have told you; for I go to prepare a place for you. If I go and prepare a place for you, I will come again and receive you to Myself, that where I am, there you may be also."

2 Corinthians 5:14–17
"For the love of Christ controls us, having concluded this, that one died for all, therefore all died; and He died for all, so that they who live might no longer live for themselves, but for Him who died and rose again on their behalf. Therefore from now on we recognize no one according to the flesh; even though we have known Christ according to the flesh, yet now we know Him in this way no longer. Therefore if anyone is in Christ, he is a new creature; the old things passed away; behold, new things have come."

Colossians 3:9–10
"Do not lie to one another, since you laid aside the old self with its evil practices, and have put on the new self who is being renewed to a true knowledge according to the image of the One who created him."

Philippians 2:13
"For it is God who is at work in you, both to will and to work for His good pleasure."

Ephesians 2:10

"For we are His workmanship, created in Christ Jesus for good works, which God prepared beforehand so that we would walk in them."

Revelation 21:2–6

"And I saw the holy city, new Jerusalem, coming down out of heaven from God, made ready as a bride adorned for her husband. And I heard a loud voice from the throne, saying, 'Behold, the tabernacle of God is among men, and He will dwell among them, and they shall be His people, and God Himself will be among them, and He will wipe away every tear from their eyes; and there will no longer be any death; there will no longer be any mourning, or crying, or pain; the first things have passed away.' And He who sits on the throne said, 'Behold, I am making all things new.' And He said, 'Write, for these words are faithful and true.' Then He said to me, 'It is done. I am the Alpha and the Omega, the beginning and the end. I will give to the one who thirsts from the spring of the water of life without cost.'"

8

THE JOURNEY CONTINUES

I've found the Gospel to be a gift that keeps on giving. Just when I thought I had it figured out, I found out how little about it I understood. I thought the Gospel was simply about Jesus saving me from my sins. I'm learning there is so much more to it.

The Gospel is showing me there is more to life than what I thought I desired. I thought getting married, having a family and a good job, and being successful would give me what I desired. I discovered I was wrong. They can't do it because they weren't made to truly fulfill me.

What I desire is to be known just as I am without being judged. I desire to be told I am loved without strings attached. I desire to know my life matters. I desire to know I have worth, value, and dignity not based on what I do, but based on who I am. I found only the Gospel can fulfill my deepest desires:

- The Gospel is God's declaration of His unconditional love for me.
- The Gospel is His statement that I am worth dying for.
- The Gospel is His statement of the value He places on having a relationship with me.
- The Gospel provides a foundation for a sense of dignity that won't change.
- None of this changes because God doesn't change.

I'm building my life on the solid foundation the Gospel provides. I'm letting go of the guilt and shame I've held onto my entire life because I'm forgiven. I'm finding a hope that will support me in the hard times and when I sin. I have hope for a future where I will finally be what I what to be.

Understanding I'm accepted and wanted because of who I am and not what I do has helped me to believe I am good enough, and what I bring to the table has value. I matter and so does my life.

I'm far from perfect. I find myself falling back into old ways of thinking and living more than I want to. However, the more I focus on the truth of the Gospel, I find myself living the abundant life promised in John 10:10.

I'm able to confront the lies I've believed for so long with what is true about me. I'm finding I turn to my addictions less and to the God of the universe who created me more to find peace where I couldn't before. My life is becoming what I've always desired it to be.

I've created an outline on the next page that lays out

the points discussed in the book. I hope this outline can bring clarity for some. For others, I hope the outline provides a way to share the Gospel. Most of all, I hope this book can be a source of hope for a better life and future for you, the reader.

GOSPEL OUTLINE TO USE WITH THOSE WHO SUFFER FROM ADDICTION

1. God loves you.
2. God created you in His image. This means you think, feel, make choices, and live in relationship.
3. We had it all in the Garden. Perfect relationship with God, His creation, each other, and ourselves.
4. Sin came into the world when Adam and Eve ate the fruit. Sin broke our relationships with God, His creation, each other, and ourselves.
5. The penalty of Sin is Death. This is why God set up the sacrificial system. There is no forgiveness of Sin without the shedding of blood.
6. God had three choices to deal with Sin. He is Holy and can't tolerate Sin. He could have started over, left us on our own, or pay the price for Sin.
7. God chose to pay the price through Jesus' death

and resurrection. Jesus' death paid the price for our Sins. Jesus rose from the grave to re-establish God's relationship with us.
8. We have to ask Jesus to forgive us of our Sins. By praying "Lord Jesus, save me, a sinner, our sins are forgiven and God's relationship with us re-established.
9. Six things become true of us when we do this: a) God becomes Lord and King in our lives; b) We are forgiven of all our sins—past, present, and future; c) We now belong to God's family which means we are accepted as we are, wanted as we are, we are redeemed, and we are restored; d) We are no longer alone in life; e) We can experience God's unconditional love; f) We have hope for today and for the future.

Introduction

1. *Pleasure Unwoven: An Explanation of the Brain Disease of Addiction,* documentary hosted by Dr. Kevin McCauley, The Institute for Addiction Study, 2006.

What Is Addiction?

1. American Psychiatric Association, https://www.psychiatry.org/patients-families/addiction
2. The National Institute on Drug Abuse, https://www.drugabuse.gov/publications/media-guide/science-drug-use-addiction-basics
3. The American Society of Addiction Medicine, https://www.asam.org/resources/definition-of-addiction
4. *Pleasure Unwoven.*
5. Gerald May, *Addiction and Grace* (New York: Harper Collins, 1988).
6. *Pleasure Unwoven.*
7. Ibid.

Who We Are: Created in God's Image

1. Larry Crabb, *Understanding People* (Grand Rapids: Zondervan, 1987).

ABOUT THE AUTHOR

Gary Ackert is a graduate of Denver Seminary and focuses his counseling on helping people break free from their addictions. A licensed addictions counselor and professional counselor, he lives in Aurora, Colorado, with his wife, Lynda.

www.garyackert.com

www.ingramcontent.com/pod-product-compliance
Lightning Source LLC
Chambersburg PA
CBHW030330100526
44592CB00010B/635